7 Mantras to Excel in Exams

Prem P. Bhalla Bsc. (Hons.)
Prolific Writer, Career Counsellor & Management Guru

Published by

F-2/16, Ansari Road, Daryaganj, New Delhi-110002
011-23240026, 011-23240027 • *Fax* 011-23240028
Email info@vspublishers.com • *Website* www.vspublishers.com

Regional Office Hyderabad
5-1-707/1, Brij Bhawan (Beside Central Bank of India Lane)
Bank Street, Koti, Hyderabad - 500 095
040-24737290
E-mail vspublishershyd@gmail.com

Branch Office Mumbai
Godown # 34 at The Model Co-Operative Housing, Society Ltd.,
"Sahakar Niwas", Ground Floor, Next to Sobo Central, Mumbai - 400 034
022-23510736
E-mail vspublishersmum@gmail.com

Follow us on

All books available at **www.vspublishers.com**

© **Copyright** V&S Publishers
ISBN 978-93-813841-8-3
Edition 2014

The Copyright of this book, as well as all matter contained herein (including illustrations) rests with the Publisher. No person shall copy the name of the book, its title design, matter and illustrations in any form and in any language, totally or partially or in any form. Anybody doing so shall face legal action and will be responsible for damages.

Printed at Param Offseters Okhla New Delhi-110020

Dedicated to

Rajiv and Rima

who are guiding their children
to excel in exams

CONTENTS

Preface	7
MANTRA 1 : KNOW YOUR DESTINATION	**9**
Step 1. Do we need exams?	10
Step 2. Where are you going?	14
Step 3. Motivation	18
MANTRA 2 : KNOW YOURSELF	**21**
Step 1. The learning process	22
Step 2. The memory process	27
Step 3. Why do we forget?	33
Step 4. Using the memory	35
Step 5. Understanding yourself	42
MANTRA 3 : ADOPT BETTER HABITS	**47**
Step 1. Studying effectively	48
Step 2. Studying habits	52
Step 3. Preparing for success	56
Step 4. A study schedule	60
MANTRA 4 : DEVELOP YOUR SKILLS	**63**
Step 1. Communication skills	64
Step 2. Language skills	69
Step 3. Reading skills	77
Step 4. Listening skills	82
Step 5. Concentration	87
Step 6. Making notes	89
MANTRA 5 : ADAPT ACCORDING TO NEED	**94**
Step 1. The wonderland of exams	95

Step 2.	School exams	99
Step 3.	College exams	101
Step 4.	Professional college exams	103
Step 5.	Writing a thesis	105
Step 6.	Know your examiner	108

MANTRA 6 : BECOME MORE COMPETITIVE		**111**
Step 1.	Competitive exams	112
Step 2.	Objective type exams	114
Step 3.	Pre-interview questionnaires	116
Step 4.	Group discussions	119
Step 5.	An interview	121
Step 6.	Medical examination	128

MANTRA 7 : GIVE OFF YOUR BEST		**130**
Step 1.	Aids to better preparation	131
Step 2.	Exam anxiety and tension	134
Step 3.	Preparing for the exam	136
Step 4.	The exam	138
Step 5.	Success in exams	143

Preface

Exams play a major role in the lives of all people. One is confronted with them on joining school. This continues up to college and even later. Entry to many vocations, both at the higher and lower levels, is dependent upon exams. Even in adult life, where learning needs to be updated regularly, exams play an important role in achieving success.

In school, students are taught a variety of subjects to equip them for adult life. However, no school teaches them how to excel in exams. Most students learn through hit-and-miss methods. Some learn it late. Many never learn it at all. It is unfortunate that youngsters are deprived of this knowledge when even those with an average IQ can excel in exams.

An effort has been made through **7 Mantras to Excel in Exams** to guide youngsters to rise step by step and excel in exams. Throughout the book exercises are given so that a person can learn through practise. After each step, **Points to Ponder** will help one perfect a technique. Many suggestions are given to help students gain confidence and a new insight to appear in exams.

Discover the 7 Mantras. Success awaits you. Go ahead and excel in your exams!

—**Prem P. Bhalla**

MANTRA 1

"Know Your Destination"

Why are you preparing and appearing for exams? What is your goal? Unfortunately, most students are unable to answer these simple questions. They fail to explain why they are studying in school or college. Those who answer explain they are doing so to obtain a certificate, degree or diploma. And why do they need these? To them, these are symbols of being educated and through these they hope to follow a reasonable vocation and achieve a respectable position in society.

But the real purpose of going to school and college is not to obtain certificates and degrees, but to get educated. The word *education* is derived from the Latin *educe*, which means *to bring forth from within*. Education is the process of preparing a person to use personal capabilities buried deep within. When one knows the purpose of education, and appears for exams that are a part of the process, the person becomes aware of his destination.

At every level of study there will be exams. Written exams, exams in practical work, viva voce, group discussions, interviews, health check-ups and a variety of other tests. Each of these is planned for a particular purpose. To prove your proficiency, you will need to understand the purpose of the exams and qualify in them. Let's proceed step by step to know our destination.

Mantra 1 : **Step 1**
Do We Need Exams?

Exam is an informal abbreviation of the word *examination*. An examination is a formal test of knowledge or ability in a subject or skill. It can also be a test of the qualifications or progress of a person.

    An exam is nothing new to any educated person. As soon as one enters a school, and learns the first few alphabets, a test soon follows. The teacher wants to ascertain whether the student has learnt what was taught. New lessons are taught as the student progresses. More difficult tests follow. The word *test* is soon replaced by the word *examination*. With frequent use, the word has simply been abbreviated to exam.

Exams Begin Early

Even before a child joins school, s/he is not spared from being tested. The mother and father of the infant take pride in making the baby sit, crawl, stand up and take its first unsteady steps. They also take pride in the child's smile and laughter, just as they are happy when the child says "Ma" or "Pa" for the first few times. The child's abilities are freely tested before friends and relatives and it is a matter of pride and happiness for the parents when the child responds.

    When children grow up and advance to higher classes, the number of subjects taught increases and so does the frequency and number of exams. There are the quarterlies, the mid-year and the final exams. That is when children question the very concept of exams. Who devised exams? Do we really need them? Is it not enough to impart the necessary knowledge and leave the rest to the person concerned? That may appear to be a reasonable way of looking at the problem, but in a civilised society it is not practical.

The Need for Exams

Let's take a look at some interesting newspapers headlines:
1. Over 120,000 to appear for the preliminary PCS exam in Uttaranchal.
2. 26,000 students apply for 120 seats in Management College.
3. Over 100,000 students sit for Common Admission Test (CAT).

Uttaranchal is a small state with only 13 districts. How many youth can possibly be recruited in the Public Civil Service to administer these districts? With 120,000 aspirants, can there be any other way to shortlist the best candidates than through an exam?

The Management College has 120 seats for various courses. Can it ever accommodate 26,000 aspirants? The Common Admission Test was introduced to ensure that the most capable youngsters were admitted into prestigious institutions that provide the future administration of the country's commerce and industry.

With a large population, and ever increasing aspirants for the top positions, exams of various kinds are the only option to select the best candidates. Exams are indeed a need and not a curse, as many make them out to be.

Survival of the Fittest

Charles Darwin suggested that there is a natural process of selection in every field all the time. In the race for selection, it is the fittest that survive. We see that happening everywhere, everyday. In every sphere of life, people compete with each other to provide better products and services. This in turn means a better life for the common man. Exams play an important role in the process of selection of the best people.

Wherever there is competition, there is bound to be some tension. Doing away with exams is not a solution to end such tension. Competition is a part of life and cannot be eliminated. To counteract the tension linked with it, the solution lies in developing the correct attitude towards exams and in understanding how to be more competitive. If one can tackle exams positively, it is a definite step towards becoming more competitive in life.

A Hurdle or Stepping-stone?

Many youth consider exams as a conspiracy to place hurdles in their path! To them every exam is a hurdle. These hurdles have been so placed that at every step some trip over them. Only a lucky few reach the finishing line. Or so such youngsters feel. This is not a positive attitude towards exams.

We need to view exams not as hurdles in life, but as stepping-stones to greater progress. Hurdles are placed at the same level. Even the finishing line is at the same level. In real life, those who succeed do not remain at the same level. They rise just as one climbs a staircase step by step. Therefore, we should perceive exams as stepping-stones to rise higher, just as we do in a staircase, slowly moving towards the top.

Look at how one makes progress in school, from kindergarten to the first, then to the second and onwards, up to the tenth and twelfth classes. Each student moves upwards as in a staircase. At the level of completing school there are many options. Each person selects an option in harmony with his skills and abilities.

Some steps are easy to climb. Others are not. It is the fittest that rise the fastest. So we should always remember that exams are not hurdles, but stepping-stones to success.

Life is an Exam

Although our immediate interest are the formal exams we encounter in everyday academic and professional life, let us not overlook that in due course everyone realises that living honourably is also an exam. Every individual undergoes tests at the hands of many people everyday. Our success depends upon our attitude. When we are positive, and take a positive outlook at what confronts us, we are successful. When we harbour doubts, we buckle.

In the same way, it is important that we learn to be positive whenever we enter an examination hall. Our attitude and confidence will take us towards success.

Exams are a Part of Life

A positive way of looking at the situation is to accept exams as a part of life. There are two elements involved in this situation: firstly, the individual who appears for the examination and, secondly, the examination. It is important that we understand all there is to know before appearing for the examination. It is equally important that we recognise our own strengths and weaknesses. When we are clear on this score, success follows.

Points to Ponder
- An exam is a formal test of knowledge and skills.
- Exams are a need of society.
- The fittest survive in this world.
- Exams help select the fittest.
- Exams are not hurdles but stepping-stones to success.
- Life too is an exam.
- A positive attitude towards exams ensures success.

Mantra 1 : **Step 2**

Where Are You Going?

Do you know where you are headed? Most students do not. They simply study to go to the next higher class and because they do not want to be labelled uneducated. They want to have certificates and degrees to prove they have gone through school and college.

Can you imagine a football or hockey field without goals on either side? How will the teams play? Will they just keep moving the ball from one end to another? How will we decide the winner? Just like the players on these fields without goals, many students keep running about aimlessly with the ball! They score no goals – because there are none before them!

Lack of Goals

A major cause of low achievement is having no goals in life. Many youngsters contend that when they reach the appropriate age, the goals will appear before them. They will then score. Unfortunately, it never happens like that. Once a child begins to study, there should be a goal towards which he gradually moves. If you have nowhere to go, you will reach just there – nowhere! Just as a boat without a rudder cannot be steered towards its destination, similarly, we cannot be successful without a goal in life. Those who set out in life with definite goals achieve much more than their friends who have no goals. This is a fact proved repeatedly.

Why We Need Goals

We need goals because they tell us where we must go. Unless we know where to go, we cannot reach there.

A very important aspect of setting goals in life is that when we accept a goal in our mind, we keep thinking about it and our mind releases a success mechanism. This success mechanism attracts individuals and circumstances that are in harmony with the goals before us. When a person decides to do a specialised course in a foreign country and makes it a burning desire in his mind in the form of a goal, he collects all the information about it gradually – details about the universities offering the course, their fee structure, the admission requirements, scholarships available etc. He studies the possibilities of employment during and after the completion of the course. If a goal were not there, none of this could be possible.

What Should Goals Be Like?

A person can have several goals for different things. However, as a student the goals that would be of immediate interest are educational goals.

First, the major goals must be fixed. It may be one such as doing an engineering degree from IIT, followed by an MBA from a top management college. Once the major goals are set, one can have smaller goals that lead to the major goals. For example, how do I prepare for the entrance exam? Should I study for it on my own, or at a good coaching institute? What institute would meet my needs? What would be the time schedule?

Even smaller goals can be bifurcated. One can have a long-term goal to be achieved in five years or more. There can be smaller goals for each year. Still smaller goals can be fixed for achievement every month or even week by week. Dedicated persons work to daily goals set every morning. As one covers the distance step by step, long stretches are covered without any fatigue. This is the magic of goal setting.

Criteria for Goal Setting

When setting goals, one must dream big. Small goals bring small results. Big goals ensure big results.

- *Goals must be challenging.* It is the element of challenge that spurs one into action and brings out the best in a person.
- *Goals must be achievable.* For example, a student who has a low interest in academics should not set a goal of becoming a college professor.

- *Goals must be flexible.* If a goal is not flexible, one can get into a rut. For example, we may set a goal to secure an engineering degree from IIT. If for some reason admission is not available, we should not lose hope, but join another institution. If they are capable, graduates from other institutions make it equally big.
- *Goals must be time-bound.* If they were not time-bound, they would lack motivation. A certain amount of work must be done in a fixed amount of time.

Ensuring We Reach Our Goal

If we want to reach our goal, it must become a burning desire within us. This is possible only when we think about it all the time.

- When we forget our goal, we must be reminded about it.
- To remind yourself about your goals, write them down in bold.
- Display your goals on a tent-card on your writing table or paste it on your dressing table.
- Discuss your goals. When you tend to forget them, your relatives and friends will remind you about them.
- Review your goals from time to time. If you are on course to achieve them, fine. If there are hurdles, consider how you can cross them. When you set out on a journey with determination, you will surely reach your destination.

Does Our Work End After Setting a Goal?

No, it doesn't. Setting a goal is only the beginning. Once a goal is set, we must prepare a plan that considers our strengths and weaknesses. It must consider the resources at hand and those that need to be arranged. The plan must also consider the hurdles we are likely to face. A timeframe must be adopted and regular evaluation of the progress must be made. Only then can we be certain that the goal will be reached.

Things to Do
1. Set long-term career and academic goals. Note them on a tent card and place them on your study table.
2. Set goals for the current year. Note down whatever you wish to achieve.
3. Break the annual goal into half-yearly goals, quarterly goals and monthly goals.
4. Learn to work on the basis of daily goals set every morning.
5. Here is an exercise you must do everyday:
   - Sit comfortably in a chair with your back straight.
   - Close your eyes. Take a deep breath.
   - Verbalise your goal. Repeat it five times.
   - Visualise that you have achieved your goal.
   - Visualise the happiness you experience after achieving the goal.
   - As you enjoy the happiness, thank God for His blessings.
   - Open your eyes, still breathing deeply.

Points to Ponder
- Most people work without any goals.
- To succeed, we must have goals.
- We can have long-term and short-term goals.
- Goals must be challenging, achievable, flexible and time-bound.
- We must remind ourselves of our goals everyday.
- We must plan to achieve our goals.

Mantra 1 : **Step 3**

Motivation

Achievers are self-starters. This means that when a person wants to achieve a definite goal, s/he has the motivation to strive for it. A motive is a goal towards which actions are directed.

To motivate means to provide one with a motive to achieve something. What could be a better motive than to excel in exams? When one adopts this as a goal, one begins to be motivated for success. With each success this motivation grows. One becomes enthusiastic, lively and involved, besides developing an absorbing interest in work.

Motivation is a strong driving force. While on the one hand it can take one to extreme religious devotion, on the other it can generate a strong feeling within a person to even disregard death. It is such motivation that compels the youth to serve at the national borders or achieve unbelievable feats. In a war a soldier is so charged up with emotion and motivation that he even disregards death.

To excel in exams is not an extreme kind of motivation. However, to excel implies to perform exceptionally well and that means to succeed. Success is one of the greatest motivators. Each success takes one a step higher to yet another success.

How do we keep ourselves highly motivated? Dream big! Visualise success at all times. Think of the things that success brings with it. Do remember that success never comes of its own accord. It results from consistent hard work. Over the years, you will realise that hard work is a small price to pay for success.

In everyday life dedicated work brings appreciation and praise. That is extremely motivating. The love of your near and dear ones is also very motivating. The affection of the parents, brothers and sisters, other relatives and friends ensures a great sense of love and belonging.

The greatest source of motivation is being in harmony with our own selves. When we are at peace with ourselves, we are motivated. A fair balance of work, pleasure and rest is relaxing. Youngsters must be involved in outdoor activities as much as they are in academics to maintain a fair balance and achieve their goals. These activities may seem of no use, but they balance the mental effort and keep one motivated.

Childhood habits make most students dependent upon their teachers or parents to supervise studies. However, students who work to excel in exams are self-motivated and do not depend upon outside supervision. They monitor their work and have their own goals to achieve. These must be achieved within a specific timeframe, though. This is possible only when we are accountable to ourselves. Those who are well motivated push themselves harder when they fail to achieve what they set out to do and earn their own rewards when they meet deadlines. Both the 'punishment' and the reward must be immediate, positive and constructive. The 'punishment' could be by way of putting in an additional hour of study or denying oneself time spent watching the TV. Similarly, the reward could be watching a movie or taking a much deserved but unscheduled break from the grind.

The finer arts like drawing, painting, music, singing and the like are often very relaxing. Even children love to indulge in them. They find concentrating on studies easier after these activities. Even when you do not play a musical instrument or sing, you can still take advantage of their motivational qualities by hearing the kind of music you find satisfying. Many persons feel that they are at their creative best after they have enjoyed fine music. Many people hear devotional music in the mornings to begin the day on the right note.

What one person may find motivating may not be so for another. Individual choices vary. One may enjoy a morning walk or jogging in the park while another may prefer to listen to devotional music at his home. The choice of music too varies with individual personalities.

Discover what motivates you best. Use your spare time for the activities that you enjoy. Listen to the kind of music that you find relaxing. Cultivate the kind of friends who give you positive vibes and suggestions. At home or away, create an atmosphere that makes you feel motivated to achieve the goals you have set for yourself.

Things to Do
1. Make a list of things that motivate you.
2. Regularly listen to your favourite music.

Points to Ponder
- Achievers are self-starters. They know how to be motivated.
- Motivation is a strong driving force.
- To be motivated, dream big. Work hard. Persevere.
- Be in harmony with your inner self.
- Find out what motivates you best.
- Keep yourself in a high level of motivation – always.

MANTRA 2

"Know Yourself"

The longest journey begins with a single step. When our goal is to succeed by excelling in exams, the first step should be to know oneself. We need to know how we learn. We need to understand how our memory works. Why do we forget? Can we improve the working of our memory? What else must we know about ourselves to move towards our goal?

Successful students have an inquisitive mind, are confident of their ability, are regular and happen to be genuinely interested in their work. They are eager learners. If one is not interested in learning a subject, no amount of coaxing or coaching can help. A high level of interest in the subject is important.

The more you know about yourself, the better your performance.

Mantra 2 : Step 1
The Learning Process

Since an exam is a formal test of one's knowledge and skills, it becomes necessary to understand how one gains knowledge or learns a skill. Both come through learning. To learn means to gain knowledge or a skill in something through study by personal effort or from a teacher or via experience. Learning also means knowledge or skills gained through systematic study in any field(s) of scholarly application. The modification of behaviour through practise, training and experience is also termed learning.

Learning Must be Part of a Person

Learning is not a temporary process. Since it implies gaining knowledge or a skill, it can only be achieved over a certain period of time and through a definite effort in the right direction. When students take a shortcut by mugging or memorising their subjects just before the exam, simply using their memory to qualify in the exams and soon thereafter forget what they had learnt, it cannot be called learning.

To understand what true learning can do for a person, Ray Palmer wrote, "Learning, if rightly applied, makes a young man thinking, attentive, industrious, confident and wary; and an old man cheerful and useful. It is an ornament in prosperity, a refuge in adversity, an entertainment at all times; it cheers in solitude, and gives moderation and wisdom in all circumstances."

How should a person go about learning? Lydia H. Sigourney suggests, "The true order of learning should be: first, what is necessary; second, what is useful; and third, what is ornamental. To reverse this arrangement is like beginning to build at the top of the edifice."

The Process of Learning

To achieve a particular level, it is important to understand how an individual learns. Let us begin when one is born. An infant learns to secure its requirements of food and security instinctively. A mother's love for her baby makes it easier. The deliberate learning process begins when a child is a few months old. Eager as all parents are to hear their baby talk to them, the first few words a child learns are "Ma" and "Pa". The baby learns them through sheer repetition. Sound is the key medium.

This indicates that one learns through phonetics initially. We have all noticed that different communities pronounce words from the same language differently. When we consider individuals from different communities, each using a different dialect, we find that their pronunciation passes from one generation to another. The child has no meaning for the words it repeats. He will learn bad words as easily as good words.

A little later, a child begins to learn through example – he copies the actions of the parents. He will learn to pick up his bottle to drink milk. In the same way, he will learn to pick up a spoon and eat. Or even pick up a small mug and take a bath. Gradually he will learn to clean his teeth. He will later begin to heed commands like picking up toys or going to sleep.

Repetitive actions are gradually stored in a child's subconscious mind. For example, when the child eats, even if he closes his eyes, the spoon containing the food will automatically go to his mouth. Activities like cleaning one's teeth do not need to be supervised. The child does them automatically. The subconscious mind has made them a part of the individual.

The child then begins to learn through coordination of activities. Learning to swim and cycle too are activities that become a part of the person once they are learnt. This ability develops fully in adult life when a person can use his legs and hands simultaneously while riding a scooter or driving a car, or performing many other activities referred to as skills.

Learning through phonetics and repetition plays an important part when a child first goes to school. Small poems and rhymes are freely used to draw his attention and gradually make them a part of his mind. At this stage the memory begins to play a role. To secure attention and appreciation, the child begins to repeat poems and rhymes. Memory continues to play a very significant part even as the child grows up. It is unfortunate that many children take it to extremes when they simply mug their lessons in the hope of writing them word for word in the exams.

Some time later, a child is taught to learn through the use of logic. For instance, 2 and 2 always make 4 or 88 is followed by 89. Or a zero is lesser than one. Learning through logic is important because this is when the child begins to learn how to reason. He now begins to appreciate that it is more important to understand and comprehend than to simply memorise a lesson. A good memory is important, no doubt. However, a proper grasp and learning of the subject is more important.

To correctly understand and learn a subject, one needs to go into greater depth. One must know who or what it is all about. Why does one need to know about this? How does one get to know it? When and where can one find the full information? When one secures the answers to these questions, knowledge of the subject becomes thorough. Although a slow process, it is a sure way to become truly knowledgeable.

One begins with simple phonetics in childhood. As one grows, new subjects are added. Additional information is gathered. At each stage there is an exam to certify that a person has qualified and truly possesses the requisite knowledge.

Selective Learning

With the increasing scope of studies, a person begins to like some subjects and dislike others. A person excels in subjects he likes, but barely passes through ones that are not particularly liked. The reason for the difference in marks is obvious – this is directly proportionate to one's interest in a subject.

A preference for a subject is a personal matter. Although individual choice is important, we can be influenced in favour of or against a subject by earlier achievements. Teachers also influence us through inadvertent remarks. Appreciation too motivates us towards one subject against the other.

A choice in favour of a subject against another may be all right at higher levels of study. At this stage one gradually moves towards specialisation. However, at lower levels, particularly up to high school, the choice is limited. One must pass in all the prescribed subjects. If one is weak in a subject, the reasons for this will need to be analysed and appropriate steps taken to correct this.

Receptivity to Knowledge

An important aspect of learning is that our receptivity to knowledge varies with exposure to information. For example, if we heard a lecture and wanted to recall it later, we would be lucky to recall one-tenth of it! But if we had noted the points during the lecture, our receptivity would improve. If we were to develop these points into notes in greater detail on reaching home, our receptivity would increase further. If we were to put this information to practical use, our grasp of the subject would become still better. Finally, our hold over a subject is best when we regularly teach it to colleagues and friends or even to students and other peers.

The way a person has trained his mind to grasp knowledge is another important factor in understanding new information. If we hear a lecture for the sheer pleasure of the way it is presented, it is soon forgotten. But if we interpret the presentation in terms of past knowledge and experience, and mentally accept or reject it according to merit, we are able to use it more beneficially.

No two individuals are alike. Similarly, their grasp of a subject also varies. Each person is guided by past experiences.

Therefore, it is important that we look back upon the way knowledge was imparted in the earlier years. There is always scope for improvement. When a person wants to forge ahead, he must be sure about his own learning responses.

> **Think it Over**
>
> *The most effective way of learning a skill is through continuous practise.*

Points to Ponder
- One gains knowledge and imbibes a skill through learning.
- Learning can add new dimensions to our personality.
- Learning begins in early childhood. It is controlled by the subconscious mind.
- One learns through phonetics, examples, repetitive actions, coordination of activities and logic.
- Learning comes from knowing the 'who', 'what', 'where', 'when', 'why' and 'how' about a thing.
- Learning gradually becomes selective.
- Receptivity to knowledge varies with personal attitude and circumstances.
- All individuals develop a personal pattern of learning.

Mantra 2 : **Step 2**

The Memory Process

To everyone preparing to appear in an exam, memory is important. It provides an important function in the learning process. All knowledge is stored in the memory. The real test lies in how well we can recall information from memory in an exam.

How Memory Works

To get the best from our memory, we must understand how the memory process works. Memory works in four steps. Let's examine each one.

1. **Attention and Selection:** A lot of primary information is generated through our senses. Everything that we see, hear, smell or touch is generating information. Innumerable messages are being received all the time. Therefore, it becomes necessary to select messages that we wish to store or to eliminate.

2. **Encoding:** The next step is to encode the selected message. It can be encoded on the basis of its sound (acoustic code), its looks (visual code) or on the basis of its meaning (semantic code). The way you encode information affects its recall.

3. **Storage:** This step aims at the storage of information in the memory. Memory can be short-term memory (STM) or long-term memory (LTM). Short-term memory is brief and transient, like a telephone number that you may remember until you dial it. Once you have used it, this is forgotten. Short-term memory holds a small amount of information for a limited period only. If short-term memory has to be converted into long-term memory, it is transferred through repetition (as with telephone numbers that are frequently used) or through association with a past memory or via regular use of the information (just as studying for a short while daily helps us learn the subject easily).

4. **Retrieval:** This refers to memory recall. It is just the opposite of encoding. Retrieval becomes easy if you follow a definite system for encoding. For example, if you use an acoustic code for encoding, you can retrieve the information if you use the same code for retrieval. Unfortunately, people use one code for encoding and another for retrieval. That makes retrieval difficult. This is of special interest to students preparing for exams.

Although the memory process has been divided into four steps, the important thing to remember is that each of these steps is connected to the others. The division is only a way of understanding the process better.

Depending upon a particular situation all of us are exposed to a lot of information through our senses all the time. This is also termed sensory memory. It comes fleetingly and vanishes just as fast. To retain what is important to us, selection is necessary. If our selection of the information is not positive, or correctly directed, a lot of useless information is accumulated. For those who have an exam as the goal for use of information later, the selection must be planned and well directed.

Memory and a Filing Cabinet

For simplicity, we could compare memory to a filing cabinet. Lots of people use filing cabinets to store their documents for later use. Let's say we receive a document today and, considering it important, decide to store it in the filing cabinet. A year later, when we require the document, if we are able to retrieve it immediately, we can say the filing system is good. But if we cannot retrieve the document when we need it, the filing system is not up to the mark.

This is exactly what happens when a person writes in an exam. If he is able to retrieve information and put it on paper within the allocated time, he scores well. If the information cannot be retrieved in time, it is obviously of no use.

To turn our filing system into a useful cabinet, we devise a definite method to retrieve a document when we need it. For example, when the filing cabinet has four drawers, we decide to place all the taxation-related files in the top drawer, the property-related files in the second drawer, the business-related files in the third drawer and all files related to miscellaneous subjects in the lowest drawer.

For further ease of retrieval, we decide that in the top drawer the income tax-related files will have a red band, those pertaining to sales tax will have an orange band and those pertaining to service tax will have a green band. These files will then be stacked colour-wise.

Again, to make it easier to find a document quickly, the files are marked year-wise. There is one file for each year. The financial year is used as the standard guideline. Within the file the documents are filed according to dates. The latest document filed will be on top.

Now if one were to ask for the sales tax final order for the year 1995–96, to reach it one would need to open the top drawer. From amongst the files with the orange band take out the file for 1995–96 and the sales tax order will be in your hand. We could reach more documents in other drawers equally fast. Indeed, a good system helps retrieve information quickly.

A Memory System

When using memory, we need to follow a system similar to the one we have for the filing cabinet. Encoding information is important in that if we use several ways, when we need to retrieve the information later, recall becomes easier. We can link things together with a variety of experiences. If one were to encode information on the basis of a single code only, retrieval would sometimes be difficult.

The procedures used for storage affect retrieval. When information is stored via connections with a variety of information, storage is lasting and easier to retrieve.

With the first three steps well taken care of, the fourth step of retrieval becomes easy and convenient. It is the retrieval of information that is important when a person appears for an exam. When the retrieval of information is good, the performance in the exam is best.

Good and Bad Memory

Why is it that some people have a good memory and others do not? Are the former gifted? No! People with a good memory are not specially blessed in any way. Their better memory is because of better observation, evaluation and training. These people use their faculties regularly. Memory is like any other body function. Use it regularly and you can depend upon it. When you do not use it, it fades and becomes worthless. Everyone can have a good memory. It all depends upon how well you put it to use.

Think it Over

The brain is an organ that can make a sophisticated computer look crude.

Improving Memory

Can a person improve his memory through use of certain drugs and medicines? This is a thought that lures many youngsters. Some pharmaceutical companies are marketing preparations that make such claims. How effective are these medications? If they were effective, would they not aid in creating super students?

The truth is that lack of certain nutrients in the food does affect one's receptivity of knowledge. Providing a balanced meal helps in overcoming this problem. It is also true that a certain amount of tension builds up during the learning process. This tension can be controlled through a positive attitude and the use of mild medications that help users physically and psychologically.

In ayurveda, Brahmi (*Bacopa monniera*) has been recommended to aid mental functions and is an important constituent of several hair oils. It is said to improve memory and lower learning stress. In homoeopathy, it is available as a plant extract and used for similar purposes. In biochemy, the salt *Kali Phos* is said to improve functions of the nerves and brain cells. There are a variety of other herbs and drugs that are similarly recommended. But these drugs are best used under medical supervision.

However, rather than rely on drugs, the best option is to ensure a balanced diet with lots of green, leafy vegetables and fruits that supply the necessary vitamins and minerals. When one eats a balanced diet, there is no need for additional supplements.

> **Think it Over**
>
> *Caffeine from a cup of coffee affects the brain within 30 minutes. Its effect lasts from 2 to 8 hours.*

Things to Do

1. To improve your memory, here is a game. You and your friends will sit in a circle. Moving clockwise, the first one begins by saying: "I went to the market and bought potatoes." The next person repeats, "I went to the market and bought potatoes and tomatoes." The third person says, "I went to the market and bought potatoes, tomatoes and cauliflower." In this way, each person adds a new vegetable to the list. The person who cannot repeat the list correctly is eliminated. The last person left is the winner. This game improves hearing, receptivity and memory.

2. Use variations of the above game. Substitute vegetables with fruits or general merchandise. You could also paraphrase the sentence: "I went travelling and visited Madrid." You can then use world capitals or cities – or whatever else you like.

3. Make a list of all the items you want to buy in the market. Put the list in your pocket. Go out and buy the items through simple recall, without looking at the list. After you

have all the items on the counter, take out the list and check what you have forgotten.

> **Points to Ponder**
> ♦ Proper understanding of the memory process is important.
> ♦ We are exposed to a variety of information all the time.
> ♦ Correct selection of information is important.
> ♦ A well-planned system of encoding helps retrieve information.
> ♦ Avoid storage of unnecessary information.
> ♦ The method of retrieval must be in harmony with the method of encoding.
> ♦ Efficient retrieval ensures good results in exams.
> ♦ Some people have a better memory than others.
> ♦ Memory can be improved through training.

Mantra 2 : **Step 3**

Why Do We Forget?

Information can be stored in long-term memory for long periods. However, sometimes we are unable to retrieve this information. In simple words, we can forget what we learnt. This is particularly important for a student because retrieval of information is important in exams.

A certain amount of 'memory decay' affects stored information. To counteract this, it is necessary to store additional information so that even if a part is lost, it is not a total loss. The basic facts about the subject are still stored.

Memory loss could be due to non-use of information, lack of proper nutrition, stress or use of medicines that may affect memory retention. To avoid loss of information, we can reinforce it through periodic revision, rethinking about it and relearning our subject. Practise helps reinforce the process of information storage.

Even when reading a book, we need to stop briefly and reflect over what we have read. This reflection helps create associations, which assists in passing information from short-term to long-term memory. If we take notes in between reading, this too helps reinforce the storage of information.

It has also been found that we remember a subject of greater interest more easily than a subject that does not interest us. Our interest makes it easier to remember things. It is also important that when we try to remember two similar issues simultaneously, we are able to differentiate between the two to avoid confusion and difficulty in memory retention.

Common Memory Features

We remember:

- Recent happenings better than those that occurred long ago.
- Special occasions better than ordinary ones.

♦ Things that we use/repeat frequently better than those used sometimes.

> **Think it Over**
>
> *Ebbinghaus, an eminent psychologist, has asserted that each additional repetition after learning a subject helps cement the information in our long-term memory. Therefore, do not stop when you feel you have learnt the subject. A little more effort will help you excel in exams.*

Things to Do

1. Make a list of all the movies that you watched in the past six months. Make another list of all the books that you read in the same period. Which list was easier to prepare? Why?
2. Can you recall the birthdays of your parents, brothers and sisters, relatives and friends? Make a month-wise list.
3. Make a list of all the teachers who taught you from the first to the sixth class. Have you missed out any? Why?

Points to Ponder

♦ A certain amount of 'memory decay' is natural.
♦ To avoid 'memory decay', reinforce the information.
♦ Revise, rethink and relearn.
♦ Practise helps reinforce storage of information.
♦ You can have a much better memory than you think.

Mantra 2 : **Step 4**

Using the Memory

To excel in exams it is not enough to gain knowledge through learning alone. It is equally important to recall the information when needed. To excel in exams is one such need. We have already discussed how the memory process works. To excel in exams we also need to know how best to develop and use our memory.

Respond to the following statements by ticking one of the options.
1. I am an observant person.
   ☐ Yes ☐ No
2. I like to look at things very analytically.
   ☐ Yes ☐ No
3. I have a good memory for faces and places.
   ☐ Yes ☐ No
4. I am able to locate my things quickly.
   ☐ Yes ☐ No
5. I am conscious of the need for a good memory.
   ☐ Yes ☐ No

If you have answered 'Yes' to all the statements, you are already using your memory well. However, if you have answered 'No' to any of them, you need to improve the use of your memory.

Good Observation

Good observation is not only an asset for good learning, but equally so for a good memory. To have good observation is to be able to notice important details. To do so one uses all the senses. It is not enough to gauge a situation visually. Whenever possible, we must employ the other senses. We must smell and hear. We must use our sense of touch. If it pertains to something edible, the sense of taste completes the observation.

The more the senses used in observing a particular situation, the better our memory about it. For instance, when a tasty dish is placed before us, its aroma and sight make our mouths water. When we eat it, our sense of touch tells us about its structure and temperature, and the sense of taste further adds to our observation. If it is a crisp dish, the crackling heard by us when eating it completes the observation. With all the five senses involved, good or bad, the dish will be retained in our memory and we will, consequently, remember it for a long time.

In comparison, how many things do we remember as we drive through the countryside? A few are remembered fleetingly. There are others that may be remembered a little longer. But none are remembered as distinctly as the dish.

In another situation, when we walk through the marketplace indulging in window-shopping, we remember much more than we did when we drove through the countryside. This is because we spend more time in observing things. We view them with greater interest. We talk about them or even try to find out the prices. We even think about these things and wonder if we can buy some of them. The longer we observe them the better our memory.

Similarly, in the process of learning and gaining knowledge, observation plays a very significant part. In a lecture, our memory depends upon what we see or hear through the lecturer. Reading reinforces whatever we have heard. Making notes further reinforces our memory of what we have learnt. In practical classes, we use our sight, hearing and sense of touch with whatever we learn. It makes learning easier and also holds our interest longer. That is why most people love to attend practical classes.

All students love outdoor learning through excursions and practical visits to factories and commercial houses. Those who have the best observation enjoy this the most and also learn more than others. Good observation is the key to a good memory.

> **Think it Over**
>
> *Efficient observation uses all the senses, not just sight.*

Analytical Observation

If one simply observes and forgets something, the subject is still memorised, but does not stay put for long. It is only when we move a step ahead and analyse what we have observed that we send the subject to our long-term memory. A little reinforcement makes it a part of our memory.

An analysis of what we observe refers to the consideration of finer details of whatever is before us. We think of it in terms of 'who', 'what', 'when', 'where', 'why' and 'how' of the situation. Whatever we observe, we compare with what we know. After comparison, we give it an appropriate place in our memory.

To understand this better, consider an example: we have all seen little children pick up a teapot with both hands and get burnt. A child does not know that a teapot is meant for hot tea. Only after being burnt does the child realise the danger of picking a teapot carelessly. Adults will always pick up a teapot carefully by the handle to avoid getting burnt. Their memory induces them to be careful, as a teapot is always associated with hot tea and the danger of getting burnt.

The learning process depends upon associating new information or knowledge with existing knowledge that is already a part of the memory. Sometimes, associations are easy to find. Many times they are not. It is the responsibility of a teacher to create associations for students. When one moves systematically from one point to another, creating associations, learning becomes easy.

What one does when making associations is not easy. Teachers have tried several ways to make it easier for students. For example, the seven colours of the rainbow are remembered easily by the word VIBGYOR, which represents the first letters of the colours – violet, indigo, blue, green, yellow, orange and red. Similarly, BHAJSAB reminds us of important Mughal rulers: Babar, Humayun, Akbar, Jehangir, Shahjahan, Aurangzeb and Bahadur Shah Zafar. Words so created are called acronyms. Acronyms are popularly used to describe organisations: WHO for World Health Organisation, ICAR for Indian Council for Agricultural Research and so on. One can use this technique to make learning easier.

Yet another similar technique is to use acrostics – sentences or poems that convey an idea or represent words from different sentences. For example, "Multiply and divide before you add or subtract" conveys an idea how mathematical operations must be done.

Rhythm, singing and repetition also help remembering and, therefore, learning. Have you noticed how quickly children learn poems and songs? It is the rhythm and repetition that helps. Even when remembering numbers, a certain amount of rhyming helps. For example, when we try to remember a telephone number, if we break it into two or three parts, it becomes easier to remember – 271 2691.

Visualising a situation is a vivid way of remembering things. Public speakers use this technique frequently and speak as if narrating whatever they are seeing. Through their descriptions they will take you from one point to another, moving between cities and even countries. Once you have the scene before you and let it seep through to the long-term memory, it becomes a part of you and can be recalled with minimal effort.

> **Think it Over**
> *Memory depends mainly on the association of thoughts and ideas.*

Remembering Faces and Places

Some people are very good at remembering faces, names and places. But many are not. The latter are always at a loss about when they met whom and are equally at sea regarding names. Those who can remember names and faces are always at an advantage and appreciated for this ability.

The best way to remember names is through repetition. When you think of a name, a face should match it. When you get in touch with each other through telephone, a face-to-face meeting or even through correspondence, the repetition of names helps make it a part of memory.

Some people have an uncanny ability to memorise places. You drive them to a place once and they know how to get there the next time. This comes from an ability of fast association with the points they pass through in their journey. Even when these people are deep in conversation during the journey, their eyes are tuned to record the points in memory.

Although the memory records messages through the five senses and stores them according to need, a very important aspect is that the memory simultaneously commands the body to respond to these messages. Have you seen players at fast ball games like squash and tennis? The player not only sees the opponent return the ball, but also anticipates where the ball is moving and coordinates the body to respond to strike the ball back. That shows how quickly the memory recognises a situation, responds to it and sends commands to different parts of the body to react.

The memory has vast potential and is capable of great feats. The secret lies in putting it to best use. If one can understand how memory works, it can play a significant role in helping a person excel in exams.

Locating Things Quickly

Most people have the habit of putting away things and not being able to locate them when required. And the more important the thing, the more difficult it is to locate it in time! This is because it has been placed away 'safely'! Being unable to locate it, people get exasperated. The more they try to locate it, the further away it goes. The next time this happens to you, do not get puzzled. And stop bothering about it. You will locate it when you stop thinking about it.

People who do not suffer from this problem are those who follow a definite system of storage and recall. One of the first few things to improve efficiency is to have a place for everything. Again, when you remove anything for use, return it to the same place after use. In this way, you can always locate things quickly without hassle. Efficient people have their books lined up on shelves and pens placed in a stand or a box. Even their cupboards have everything neatly in place. Their personal vehicles too, be it a cycle, scooter or car, will be well maintained and parked in a way that will not create a hindrance for anyone.

What has all this to do with our memory? When you are well organised with things, you will also be well organised with your thoughts and with what you learn. When you can locate your books, notes, stationery and other items quickly, you will also be able to locate necessary information quickly. Good organised behaviour is an important step in learning to excel in exams.

Memory Consciousness

When a person is aware of the need for proper utilisation of information and knowledge to excel in exams, one becomes conscious of the need for good memory. Like any other body function, it must be cared for. Good health, proper nutrition and sufficient rest are important to ensure good memory.

Those with a good memory have keen observation, are quick to analyse what is good for them and immediately associate it with an existing experience. If they cannot comprehend the information immediately, they take notes and revise them later to make the information a part of their memory.

These people are aware of the fact that information gradually fades away with disuse. This makes it necessary that whatever information is important must be reinforced periodically through revision. A subject learnt in the earlier part of the year must be revised so that the information remains within current memory until the exams are over.

When recall of some information is required regularly, through use it becomes a part of the active memory of a person. Even a roadside tyre repair boy knows the specific tyre pressure for a cycle, a scooter, a motorcycle, and for different makes of cars and for trucks and buses. This is learnt through repetition of tasks or information.

Things to Do

1. To check your ability of observation, open your fridge, note all that it contains and close the door. Write down the details of all the items you saw in the fridge. Compare your list with the contents. Did you get all the items right?
2. Make a list of all students in your class. Did you get all the names right? Make a similar list a week later. Is there any improvement?

Points to Ponder

- Memory plays a crucial role in helping us excel in exams.
- People with keen observation are good learners.
- While making observations use as many senses as possible.
- Analysing what one observes helps in remembering details.
- Learn to create associations of thoughts to gain knowledge quickly.
- Remembering faces and places is no mystery. You too can do it.
- Have a place for everything. You will then locate things quickly.
- Always be conscious of the need for a good memory.

Mantra 2 : **Step 5**

Understanding Yourself

Education and the learning process affect the personality of an individual. Therefore, it is necessary to understand ourselves. And unless we do so, it will neither be possible to derive the best from the learning process, nor put in our best performance in exams.

Respond to these statements by ticking one option.
1. I enjoy good health.
   ☐ Yes ☐ No
2. I am careful about my food and nutritional requirements.
   ☐ Yes ☐ No
3. I am conscious of the need to exercise for good health.
   ☐ Yes ☐ No
4. I am conscious of the need for rest, relaxation and sleep.
   ☐ Yes ☐ No
5. I am fortunate to have family support in my efforts to study.
   ☐ Yes ☐ No

If your answer to any of the above questions was "No", you need to look into that aspect of your life immediately. You have goals to achieve and a long way to go. Good health will be your best asset.

Good Health

Good health is a prerequisite for any progress in life. Unfortunately, most youth take health for granted. Since they have a vast reservoir of energy within, they think it will last forever. Little do they realise that nature has its own ways. If one fails to live a disciplined life, the reservoir of energy soon dries up.

Modern youngsters are fortunate in that, thanks to smaller families, parents are able to provide better care for their children. Despite this, there is greater obesity amongst the youth, which leads to several problems. More youngsters are now suffering from ailments like diabetes. While parents are increasingly indulgent, youngsters are stressed. There is greater abuse of tobacco and liquor amongst youth. Many suffer from breathing and digestive problems.

A person can be healthy only by developing health consciousness. The mind is the master control centre of the body. Good health can be achieved by feeding the mind with positive thoughts. If you wish to be healthy, you need to feed the mind with thoughts about good health. So think about good health. Talk about good heath. Learn to be happy. Happiness and good health are interconnected. When you become conscious of the need for good health, you become conscious of the many factors that make or mar your health. Learn to use those that benefit you and eliminate those that do not. Good habits ensure good health.

> **Think it Over**
> *The brain is the largest consumer of energy. Lack of nutrition affects it quickly.*

Nutritional Requirements

All youngsters assert that they eat the best. Even parents confirm that they provide the very best they can afford. Few youngsters think in terms of their daily diet being the cause of most of their problems. Yet, unknown to them or the parents, many youngsters feel tired, have strained eyesight and are unable to concentrate on studies primarily because of the wrong kinds of food. Hogging on costly junk food is no assurance against malnutrition. What's important is a good diet.

One must eat a balanced diet rich in protein, with some carbohydrates and a little fat. Milk, fruits and vegetables that provide bulk and essential vitamins and minerals must form a major portion of the diet. Food must be eaten unhurriedly and chewed thoroughly. Work and worry must be taboo at mealtimes. Overeating must be avoided. Snacks and beverages should never replace regular meals. And we must drink lots of pure clean water as often as possible.

Exercise and Good Health

Although hard to believe, there are more lazy youth today than ever before. Television is one major cause for this lethargy. Scooters and motorcycles are replacing bicycles. A greater number of home appliances, a more comfortable lifestyle and changed attitudes are all responsible for increasing laziness amongst youth.

Exercise affects two important functions in the human body – breathing and circulation of blood. And both affect other functions in the body. But our immediate concern is their effect on learning. The lack of both affects the learning process adversely. Poor breathing implies poor quality of blood; poor circulation means poor nutrition for our mind and other organs. Can we then achieve our full potential to become good learners?

Exercise helps increase the capacity of our lungs. The deeper we breathe, the more oxygen we provide the body. Deep breathing is very stimulating – both physically and mentally. Better circulation too ensures that nutrients reach every part of the body. It also improves the removal of waste matter from the blood, helps keep the mind active and prevents one from tiring quickly.

Youngsters who play outdoor games get enough exercise. But with many schools unable to provide playing facilities, a sedentary lifestyle cannot be justified. Walking, swimming, jogging and cycling provide good exercise. Even within the home we can exercise to ensure good health.

> **Think it Over**
> *Most of us use only two-thirds of our lung capacity to breathe.*

Rest, Relaxation and Sleep

Youngsters tend to adopt two opposing attitudes: excessive rest and sleep amounting to sheer laziness, on one hand, and extreme activity totally ignoring rest, relaxation and sleep, on the other. Both attitudes are wrong.

Just as we need to work hard, we also need proper rest, relaxation and sleep. This is nature's way of recharging the human body. Even for adults, brief rests in between work promote efficiency. Likewise, good restful sleep helps recharge the system for another day of hard work.

Relaxation and sleep are of significant importance when considering their impact on exams. Students tend to cut out these, particularly at exam time, to gain additional time for revision. This is wrong. Relaxation improves human performance and should not be totally avoided. Similarly, sleep has a positive role to play in recharging the whole body and gearing it for exams.

There are instances when students who did not rest and sleep then totally blacked out during exams. Can you afford to be in such a situation? If not, do not overlook the need for rest, relaxation and sleep.

> **Think it Over**
> *A hot bath half-hour before sleep ensures deeper and longer sleep.*

Family Support and Studies

The need for family support must not be underestimated. Understanding parents, brothers and sisters ensure that we can concentrate in our work without undue interruptions. Indeed, the emotional support and encouragement given by the family helps greatly in preparing us better for exams. Learning and exams have much to do with the mind, which controls the body functions just as it does our emotions. Emotions are greatly affected by family relationships. When relationships are congenial, we feel happy. If there is discord, we are disturbed. Therefore, emotional health is as important as physical health.

All kinds of work produce a certain amount of tension. So do studies. Exams cause greater tension because of the anxiety associated with them, particularly just prior to the exams. To cope with this tension family support is always welcome. To gain family support, share your goals and let them know about your study plans and schedules. Make your family a part of your work and tell them you cannot reach your goals without their support. Let them take pride in your achievements. With family support you will go a long way.

Things to Do

1. Make two lists – one of your good habits and another of bad habits. Resolve to strengthen the good habits and overcome the bad ones.
2. Make a list of what you eat for breakfast, lunch and dinner. Do you think your diet is balanced?
3. Make it a habit to do some physical exercise daily.

Points to Ponder

- To make steady progress we must understand ourselves.
- Good health is important for all progress in life.
- Despite better health consciousness and facilities, more youngsters suffer from health problems.
- A balanced diet provides the nutritional requirements of the body.
- Exercise is as important as good nutrition.
- Avoiding rest, relaxation and sleep is like burning a candle at both ends.
- Family support ensures better emotional health to achieve our goals.

MANTRA 3

"Adopt Better Habits"

The personality of an individual depends upon his habits, which can be both good and bad. Whereas good habits help an individual, bad ones let him down. It is no different when a person sets out to excel in exams.

Once a person has set definite goals, one must understood how the learning process works and, also, where one stands in achieving these goals. When setting out on a long journey, the next step is to adopt better habits as they affect an individual's learning. We need to have good study habits in order to learn effectively and achieve success. Once these steps are taken, we will be able to develop a good study schedule. This will take us closer to our goal – to excel in exams.

Mantra 3 : **Step 1**

Studying Effectively

A variety of subjects are taught in schools and colleges. Unfortunately, nobody teaches students how to study effectively. If this single aspect were well understand, the overall performance of students would improve. Even those with an average IQ would excel in studies.

In the present ultra-competitive world where we need to be fully aware of many things, it is important we realise it is not enough to work harder. It is more important to work *smarter*. For effective learning, we should know how to achieve more in lesser time and with lesser effort. Before we learn how to improve the effectiveness of our learning processes, let us assess where we stand today. Answer these simple questions by ticking one of the options:

1. Do I have a timetable for my study routine?
   ☐ Yes ☐ No
2. Is my place of study comfortable?
   ☐ Yes ☐ No
3. Do I have a comfortable chair and table to sit and work on?
   ☐ Yes ☐ No
4. Is my place of study well lit?
   ☐ Yes ☐ No
5. Is my place of study free from interruptions?
   ☐ Yes ☐ No

If the answer to any of the above questions is 'No', your place of study is not right. You will need to take appropriate steps to ensure that all the answers soon turn to 'Yes'.

Timetable for Study

A proper timetable for studies is important. When we adopt a timetable, we place a definite schedule of action before us. We prepare ourselves mentally to meet it. A timetable removes the uncertainty from what we need to do or not do. We already have a plan for you, but *you* have to implement it. Since variations are a part of life, any plan should be flexible enough to absorb these variations. A certain time cushion or margin is essential in any schedule.

How do we plan a timetable for personal study? This is done much like a school or college timetable. You have no control over that timetable, since the school or college authorities prepare it. But you do have control over your own timetable, which should be planned so that you can revise what you study in the day. You can prepare additional notes about what you study. The time can also be utilised for doing homework on the subject. If more than one subject has been studied, you can divide your time amongst them.

Place of Study

A comfortable place of study is important to improve the learning process. Have you noticed that the offices of top managers are done up to provide the maximum comfort? All top managers draw both extensively and intensively from their learning and experiences to promote their work. A comfortable atmosphere helps produce better work.

As a student, you may not have an exclusive room for study. If you do have one, it is an advantage. However, any place in the house that is available and where you feel comfortable is all right. Don't mistake studying while lying in bed as a comfortable place to study. A bed is comfortable to sleep, not study! Comfort refers to the ambience. Each time you enter the study area, your mind should automatically switch to the study mode. Then you will not need to concentrate on bringing the mind there.

Comfortable Furniture

It is surprising to see the number of students who do not have a proper chair or table to sit and study. Some students study while lying in bed, sitting on a sofa, a diwan or a stool and using a low table. Is it any surprise that they do not perform as well as they possibly can?

One needs to sit on a comfortable chair with a straight back. Have you noticed that when you want to be attentive, you sit up and straighten your spine? This improves concentration. When not attentive, you slouch and the spine curves. This lowers your concentration. When studying, you must be attentive and concentrate. Have a comfortable chair with a straight back. If you cannot afford one, use a chair from the dining set.

The table must be just right for you to work on. A standard writing table is 30 inches from the ground. At this level one can read and write comfortably. If you can have a table of your own, it is fine. If not, use the dining table as an alternative. However, you will need to adjust your study schedule so that it does not clash with the family dining time.

Lighting

Proper lighting in the place of study is very important. Just as you cannot cook well in a dark kitchen, you cannot study well if the area is not well lit. Many students complain of headaches and strained eyesight. Both are due to poor lighting conditions. Unfortunately, many classes in schools and colleges are not well lit. That may not be within your immediate control, but the lighting in your study place at home is definitely within your control.

A well-lit study place must ensure that the light falls upon the book you are reading or writing on. The lighting must be good enough for you to see the book and copybook simultaneously. Besides, the light should not fall on your face while studying. This can affect eyesight and cause headaches. It also reduces concentration.

Think it Over

Study at the same time each day. Your biological clock will set accordingly and result in better work.

Interruptions

If you want your study time to be a learning time, there should be no interruptions. Your timetable should be so planned that there will be the least number of interruptions. If you usually attend to the telephone or the doorbell, ask some other family member to do so when you are studying. Do not let study time interfere with mealtimes. It is not possible to study and eat simultaneously.

Friends are a common cause of interruptions. If you are serious about studies, tell your friends when you will be studying and not be available to them. But it would be good to reserve some part of your schedule for friends. You can tell them that you will only be available at that time. You will also do well to acquaint family members about your study time. Interruptions from family members can be as bad as that from friends.

Things to Do

1. Make a timetable for your study at home. Revise it in a few days to suit your convenience.
2. Check the lighting of your study place. If the light is insufficient, change the source or purchase a table lamp.

Points to Ponder

- Even average students can excel if they study effectively. Ensure the effectiveness of your work.
- A timetable places a definite schedule of action before you.
- The place of study sets one's mood for study. Make your place of study comfortable.
- A comfortable chair and table are necessary for effective study.
- A well-lit study place prevents eyestrain, headache and stress.
- Avoid interruptions at study time. They are major time wasters.

Mantra 3 : **Step 2**

Studying Habits

Anything we do repeatedly becomes a habit. Everything begins with a thought. The thought is then converted into action. Actions that are repeated become a habit. Habits can be good and bad. Good studying habits are important if we want to excel in exams. But first, we must understand what constitute good studying habits.

Let us try to assess where we stand today by answering the questions listed here:

1. Do I sit erect and study comfortably?
   ☐ Yes ☐ No
2. Do I enjoy studying?
   ☐ Yes ☐ No
3. Can I concentrate on my subject of study?
   ☐ Yes ☐ No
4. Do I try to understand the subject rather than simply memorise it?
   ☐ Yes ☐ No
5. Do I get bored easily?
   ☐ Yes ☐ No

If the answer to any of the above questions is 'No', your study habits are improper. You will need to take appropriate steps to ensure all the answers become 'Yes'.

Studying Comfortably

Unless one is comfortable at study time, one cannot study effectively. Some walk around as they read aloud and try to memorise lessons. Others slouch in a couch and read. A few feel that studying while lying in bed is most comfortable. None of these ways are very effective. Even if you have been successful on earlier occasions using these methods, you can discover better ways to study.

The best way is to sit erect on a chair with a straight back and a table of an appropriate height before you. Now, you can make notes comfortably or even do the written exercises. If reference material is required, you can have this handy nearby. Your effort should be to ensure that at study time you are sitting just as you would when appearing for exams. In this way, recalling information will be easier.

Enjoying Studies

If you do not like studying, you cannot learn. And if you cannot learn, you cannot succeed in exams. Your capability to learn is directly proportional to the interest you have in a subject. When you are interested in a subject, you will enjoy studying it. Therefore, interest is very important and it will help you feel motivated to study.

With the wide variety of subjects one needs to study till the high-school level, it is necessary to keep oneself equally interested in all subjects. While you may excel in your favourite ones, do not lag behind in others since this will affect the overall results. Later, as you move to senior school and then college, maintaining interest may not be difficult, as you are free to choose what you wish to study.

Concentration

Lack of concentration is a common reason for poor learning skills. Many students complain that they sit down to study, but find it hard to concentrate on the subject. Thereby, they fail to grasp the subject. The first step in avoiding this problem is to have an appropriate place to study, which ensures you get into the right spirit for study. Our minds associate an activity with a particular place, so having a proper study area makes it easier to concentrate.

The next step towards promoting concentration is an interest in the subject. The greater the interest, the better the concentration. Having interest in subjects of your choice is easy. But this is not so for all subjects. In that case, you should consider the usefulness of the subject and mentally remind yourself why the subject is so important for you. If nothing else, your overall average depends upon how well you do in the subject. Personal motivation helps develop concentration.

When you cannot concentrate on a subject, read it, think about it and make notes. As you expose the memory to more of the subject, and for longer periods, you begin to understand it better. You also begin to appreciate its utility for you. Your notes will help you revise the subject faster, which is a great asset during exams.

> **Think it Over**
>
> *To improve concentration, create an interest in the subject.*

Understanding the Subject

When some people are unable to comprehend a subject, their next choice is to memorise it. They read loudly and through sheer repetition try to memorise it. Some succeed in doing so and during the exams, they write it ad verbatim. But these students never really learn the subject or benefit from the memorising. Soon after the exams, they forget whatever they memorised.

The real solution lies in understanding the subject. One must appreciate why it is important. If you follow the correct study techniques, it will not be difficult to understand the subject. But you cannot do this in a hurry. So take it easy. Let everything seep into your mind slowly. If you are impatient, you cannot learn. You will need to gradually master the techniques followed by all good students. We will discuss these subsequently.

Boredom

A person who has no interest in the work at hand gets bored easily. People often say they are not in the right mood. Can a person who has something to achieve wait until he gets into the right mood? A mood reflects one's mental state. In the positive sense, the person could be elated. In the negative sense, he could be depressed. Either way, one cannot give in to being moody.

Boredom is a state of mind. When we have something to achieve, we need to shake ourselves out of this boredom and act. Correct action will ensure results. When you have goals before you, and a schedule to achieve them, you cannot wait for inspiration. This must come from within you. You must learn to keep yourself in a high state of motivation, which is a dynamo that can always keep you charged.

Things to Do

1. Make a list of your good and bad habits. In what category did you list your study habits? How do you plan to change your bad habits into good ones?
2. Organise your textbooks, exercise books and writing stationery for a better study atmosphere.
3. Set specific deadlines to improve study habits.

Points to Ponder

- Habits are building blocks for both success and failure.
- Good study habits ensure positive results.
- A comfortable place of study sets the mood for study.
- Those who enjoy studying learn quickly.
- Concentration helps you study effectively.
- Memorising or mugging is not a good alternative to having a proper grasp of the subject.
- Boredom is a state of mind. Achievers do not wait for inspiration.
- Good study habits ensure steady learning everyday.

Mantra 3 : **Step 3**

Preparing For Success

Are you prepared to become a successful student? Everyone would like to respond with an emphatic "Yes"! But success does not come just for the asking. You have to work for it. Here are a few statements. Tick what you consider is your proper option.

1. I am self-disciplined.
   ☐ Yes ☐ No
2. I tackle problems and assignments systematically.
   ☐ Yes ☐ No
3. I always read directions before taking up an assignment.
   ☐ Yes ☐ No
4. I like to complete assignments in time.
   ☐ Yes ☐ No
5. Whenever in doubt, I like to check facts.
   ☐ Yes ☐ No

If your response is not "Yes" to all statements, you need to understand yourself better. Make improvements where necessary. This will ensure your success.

Self-discipline

The first step to achieve success is self-discipline. Those who cannot live with a certain discipline will not succeed. The entire universe functions on the basis of a discipline enforced by the great force we call God. The planets move according to a predetermined system. Climatic changes come and go in a definite rhythm. The animal and plant kingdoms respond the same way year after year. If this discipline broke down there would be chaos. All life would soon perish.

Human success too depends upon discipline. This must begin with each one of us personally. And this requires we understand ourselves well. Since no two individuals are alike, we need to appreciate that we are a combination of both good and bad. So we must be aware of our strengths as well as weaknesses. This done, we can give greater emphasis to our strengths and take steps to transform our weaknesses into strengths.

Tackling Assignments Systematically

The immediate assignment before you is to learn how to succeed and excel in exams. For this, you will need to do two things. First, know yourself well. Second, learn to prepare well for the exams.

To know yourself better, you must understand that the period between childhood and adult life is a trying one for all youngsters. Although our tests and exams begin in childhood, they become more important as we enter adolescence. We need to set and plan academic and career goals in life. Therefore, it is important that students take their own physical and emotional changes in stride and focus on a well-balanced physical and academic growth.

At this stage of life youngsters seek answers to many disturbing problems. It is advisable that they read good books on the subject. Besides books from other publishers, there is *Teens to Twenties*, published by *Pustak Mahal*. A good book will answer most of their queries and put their troubled minds to rest. They can then concentrate on their upward journey to success.

The academic aspects of success are discussed in this book. By the time you complete reading and understanding the fundamentals of how to excel in exams, you will be well on your way to success.

Reading Directions

Seeking directions is part of any journey towards one's destination. Nobody is born learned. Everyone needs to learn. The problem is not that correct directions are not available. The real problem is many youngsters think they know it all! They feel, 'We do not need directions'. But when they move out without directions, many times they travel a long way before realising they have been walking on the wrong path.

Seeking and understanding directions really means to know what is expected in a particular assignment. A few people develop the habit of reading directions carefully. Most do not. In exams there are many failures simply because the directions have not been correctly understood. Questions are wrongly interpreted and answered. When that was not what the examiner desired, there is no reason why he will give the student good marks.

Timely Completion

Completing an assignment on time does not qualify a person for higher marks. But it does reflect the person's attitude and attitude towards time. If you want to excel in exams you need to remember that all exams are time-bound. It does not matter whether a person is appearing for the half-yearly exams in the school or college or appearing for special competitive exams that lead one to great careers – all exams are time-bound. We must remember this fact very clearly.

When the exams are time-bound, we cannot overlook the fact that the need for preparation is also time-bound. From the day we decide to appear for a particular exam, each day must have something to show for our preparations towards success in the exams. The proverbial race between the hare and the tortoise may have been repeated too often. However, the tortoise continues to remind us of the need to cover some part of the journey each day. This is all about good time management. The habits that you adopt about time now will take you a long way even in your professional life.

Checking Facts

Nobody knows everything. Not even teachers. If you are ignorant about something, don't hesitate to seek information. If you have no one you can ask, look up the facts in books. A library is a treasure house of information. The Internet is the modern treasure house of information worldwide.

People who excel in exams have an inquiring mind. They love asking questions and collecting information about whatever they wish to learn. This is a habit with those who wish to succeed. On their bookshelves, good learners must have reference books like a good dictionary, an atlas, a thesaurus, a book of synonyms and antonyms, and a book of proverbs and quotations. These are not meant to adorn the bookshelf, but for quick and ready reference. There is no one so learned that he cannot learn more.

> **Think it Over**
> *It is easier to hold attention for a physical activity than for a mental one. While studying is a mental activity, writing is a physical one. Mix studying and writing activities.*

Things to Do
1. Write five things you will do to become more successful than what you are presently.
2. Ask five people how they rate you on time management. Do they rate you as one who has regard for time?

Points to Ponder
- Self-discipline is the first step to success.
- Begin by understanding yourself well.
- A systematic approach to work helps one succeed.
- Seeking directions is part of the journey towards one's destination.
- Completing work in time reflects good time management.
- Nobody knows everything. Don't hesitate to check facts.

Mantra 3 : **Step 4**

A Study Schedule

You must have a definite timetable for study at home. This can be drawn in sync with the school or college timetable. It must have provisions for homework, making revision of what was taught that day and also include some time for making notes. On days when there is no school or college, additional time can be allocated for notes and revision.

An important part of the study schedule should be reserved to improve personal skills. An individual differs from others by virtue of his personal skills – the more the skills, the more capable a person. You need to have a variety of skills for all-round development. We will discuss those relevant to study and exams in the chapters that follow.

Most parents lay too much emphasis on academics. But all work and no play make Jack a dull boy, indeed. Any work schedule must have provision for both study and leisure. The leisure period could be utilised for indoor and outdoor activities. The important thing is to have a fair balance between study and leisure.

What about the duration of the study period? Many parents insist that after some relaxation, the rest of the time must be spent studying. The schedule will necessarily vary with the level of study, but there are certain criteria to be remembered when planning a work schedule.

Do not have long periods of study at a stretch. Parents take pride that their child studies for three hours at a stretch. But this is not right. After a certain period of study, the mental receptivity of a child diminishes. When the child continues studying even after this, complete benefits do not accrue from such study.

A child's receptivity for a subject is optimum for 40 to 45 minutes. This is why all classes in school and college are planned for this length of time. At home the maximum period one should study a subject is for one hour. Then, a short break of 10 minutes is helpful. The child may need to drink a glass of water, have a cup of tea or even visit the toilet.

But the break should not be utilised for activities like playing or watching television, which distract one and make it difficult to return to study. A separate time must be allocated for these activities. The basic purpose of the break is to give the eyes and muscles some rest. Sitting in one posture can be tiring and some physical tension builds up. A little movement relieves the muscles.

A change of subject of study also serves to relieve fatigue. For example, if one were studying history, a switch to mathematics is welcome. Similarly, a change in study activity can also be useful. If one were doing writing work, reading will then help improve receptivity. Doing graphic work can also be very relaxing.

Alternating the kind of activity we do is very helpful in improving receptivity. But no two individuals respond in the same way. So every student must decide what is most suitable for him or her in particular circumstances. With personal preferences in mind, a suitable study schedule can be made. More important than the schedule is the resolution to follow it religiously. Only then can we derive maximum benefit from it.

The SQ3R Formula

Many educators recommend the SQ3R formula for effective study. Simply explained, this formula is:

1. **Survey:** Get to know what you need to learn.
2. **Question:** Why do I need to learn it? How can I learn it? Where and when can I get all the information?
3. **Read:** Read as much as you can on the subject. The more the better.
4. **Recite:** This means repetition, which helps retention of information. It also implies taking notes.
5. **Revise:** Periodic revision of a subject helps one learn better.

> **Think it Over**
>
> *Long periods of study deplete chemicals that affect processing of information in the brain. Even with breaks of 10 minutes after every hour of study, one should not exceed four hours of non-stop study.*

Things to Do

1. Revise the timetable of your study at home keeping in view the suggestions discussed in this chapter.
2. How do you rate your receptivity to learning: good, fair or bad? How do you plan to improve it?

Points to Ponder

♦ A definite timetable for study at home is important.
♦ The timetable must be balanced for both study and leisure.
♦ Some time must be allocated for improving personal skills.
♦ Do not have long unbroken periods of study. This hampers learning.
♦ Alternate different kinds of activities for better receptivity.
♦ Alternate different subjects for a balanced interest in studies.
♦ All individuals are unique and respond differently to studies.
♦ Keep the study plan in harmony with personal preferences.

MANTRA 4

"Develop Your Skills"

An individual is known by his abilities. These abilities depend upon his learning and skills. In turn, these depend upon his habits and attitudes.

For the person who has identified his destination and understands himself, the next step is to develop the skills that lead to success. Whatever we are happens to be the result of how our inherited characteristics reacted with the circumstances we faced. Finally, an individual becomes a symbol of both good and bad. Everyone is endowed with both strengths and weaknesses.

To develop skills, one needs to reinforce strengths and steadily overcome weaknesses. This is a gradual process. When one gets down to it, success follows ultimately.

Mantra 4 : **Step 1**

Communication Skills

Earlier, we discussed the fact that an exam is a test of how well a person has learnt a particular subject or skill. To qualify in the exam it is not sufficient to only learn a subject or skill. It is equally important to properly communicate to the examiner what we have learnt. This requires a variety of communication skills.

Through these questions, let's assess where we stand:

1. Do I write legibly and neatly?
   ☐ Yes ☐ No
2. Do I have good knowledge of the language I communicate in?
   ☐ Yes ☐ No
3. Can I speak what I want to convincingly?
   ☐ Yes ☐ No
4. Can I write what I wish to communicate convincingly?
   ☐ Yes ☐ No
5. Do I possess the necessary graphical skills?
   ☐ Yes ☐ No

If the answer to any of the above questions is 'No', your communication skills are not up to the mark. You must take appropriate steps to ensure all the answers become 'Yes'.

> **Think it Over**
>
> *The ability to communicate well overshadows all other skills.*

Writing Legibly and Neatly

One of the first few skills taught to little children is writing legibly and neatly. Initially, children are compelled to do so. With time, when nobody checks them, many begin to scribble. This is unfortunate. A good neat handwriting is a great asset if you wish to score well in exams. Even if you know your subject well and answer all questions correctly, can you blame the examiner for deducting marks if he cannot comprehend what you have scrawled? This is a common problem with underachievers – their handwriting lets them down.

Neatness in presentation is equally important. If the handwriting is legible, but the presentation is not neat, the examiner is bound to give fewer marks. The situation may not be as stark in technical subjects where facts are important and marks are granted on the basis of the technical information. But neatness is definitely important when details count, as in language and arts subjects.

To practise and improve handwriting and neatness, an ideal time is when you prepare notes. Take time over them. They will give you an opportunity to write legibly and neatly. Besides, when they are well written, you will find it a pleasure to go through them when you need to make revisions just before exams.

Think it Over

Handwriting is an art open to any amateur, for the delight he gets from it himself and the further pleasure he gives to others.
—*Lewis Mumford*

Knowledge of the Language

To communicate effectively it is necessary that we possess a good knowledge of the language we speak or write. Most of us think we possess a good knowledge of our language. But experience indicates this is not always so. There is great difference in communicating through the spoken word and the written word. While speaking, pronunciation and the tone of voice can significantly change meanings. Likewise, facial expressions and gestures affect communication.

When a message is put on paper, possible variations in meaning are restricted within certain limits. The intention of the written word is to convey specific information. So, practical knowledge of the language is important, which we will discuss later.

Speaking Convincingly

Not all exams require you to speak convincingly. However, particularly at higher levels, the ability to speak convincingly is a great asset. Even otherwise, in normal adult life, all those who possess the ability to speak well achieve greater success than those who don't.

To speak convincingly, besides knowledge of a subject of study, you need to have sufficient confidence. Speaking one to one is not difficult. But when speaking to a group, many people blank out. Debates and declamation contests in schools help students overcome the fear of speaking to bigger gatherings. Speaking skills are not inherited. One learns this through practise.

If you need speaking skills as part of your career requirements, it is best to begin early. Children who overcome stage fright in the early years develop greater confidence in adult life. Even if you missed out learning this in your school days, you can still learn to speak confidently.

Communicating through the Written Word

Once you know the language well, it should not be difficult to communicate through the written word, which is definitely easier than communicating via speech. When writing, one is under less pressure. One can think and frame sentences and even revise them. You can also experiment with words – a liberty you cannot take when speaking.

When the purpose of written communication is to respond to the examiner's questions about a particular subject, good knowledge of the subject is important. Once you know your subject well, it is equally important how well you communicate this by using the appropriate words and style. Never try to be pedantic. The purpose of an exam is to judge your knowledge and ability. The examiner will gauge this through your answer.

To make the answer convincing and effective, you must remember the three Cs: clear, concise and convincing. In essence, your answers must be very clear and to the point. Clarity of thought immediately tells the examiner that you know what you are writing about. When the answers are concise, the examiner knows you are not using frills to cover up any lapses on your part. When the answers are clear and concise, it is not difficult to make them convincing. Good marks follow automatically.

> **Think it Over**
>
> *One is not born with communication skills. They are learnt.*

Graphic Skills

Few youngsters possess good graphic skills. These skills may not be necessary for several subjects, but there others like botany, zoology, chemistry and physics where graphic skills help you illustrate written answers with diagrams.

Each day, graphic skills are becoming more important as subjects are being added where diagrams help impart knowledge quickly. It is said a good picture is worth a thousand words. A diagram accompanying a written exercise serves a similar purpose. It immediately conveys to the examiner that you know your subject well.

Graphic skills also help a student in preparing good notes. When diagrams accompany written notes, it becomes easy to revise the subject quickly before exams. Many subjects that do not need a diagram can still be learnt quickly through diagrammatic presentations. Even leading magazines use this method to illustrate an important event.

The only way to learn graphic skills is through practise. Use sketches and diagrams wherever you feel they improve understanding of the subject.

> **Think it Over**
>
> On an average, 9% time is spent in writing, 16% in reading, 30% in speaking and 45% in listening.

Things to Do

1. If your handwriting is not good, now is the time to start improving it. Purchase a four-line exercise book and practise writing in it. What should you write? This is a common question because you cannot write your class-work in it. To practise good handwriting, write the sentence: *The quick brown fox jumped over the lazy dog.* All the alphabets appear in this sentence.
2. Read the newspaper daily to improve language skills.
3. To improve speaking skills, read jokes from a book, magazine or newspaper. Repeat it to friends and family members. It will ensure practise and help build speaking confidence.

Points to Ponder

- Communication skills are necessary to convey what one has learnt.
- Good handwriting speaks loudly about one's personality.
- Unless one knows the language fluently, a message cannot be conveyed convincingly.
- The ability to speak convincingly reflects your self-confidence.
- Speaking skills are learnt through practise.
- Communicating through the written word is very important in exams.
- Graphic skills improve communication.

Mantra 4 : **Step 2**

Language Skills

One necessarily needs to communicate through a language. Even when one is unable to speak or hear, one communicates through sign language. The visually handicapped use Braille to read and write.

English continues to be the most popular language all over the world. It is a colourful language. If you know English, you can find your way almost anywhere in the world. It has around two million words expressing varying shades of meaning. How large is your vocabulary? Some have a vocabulary of a few thousand words. Most people go through life with a vocabulary of a few hundred words only!

Every individual has two kinds of vocabulary: receptive and active. A receptive vocabulary includes words that you understand when you hear or read them. The active vocabulary includes words you use to express yourself when you speak or write. There is a big difference between the two!

An ideal opportunity for you to strengthen your vocabulary and power of expression is by reducing the gap between your receptive and active vocabulary. Include more words you understand in active speech and writing use. Take interest in words. They make a fascinating study. Have a dictionary as your constant companion. Don't hesitate to check any word that is not very clear to you. Try to learn new words everyday. Make a note of these and review them periodically.

Buy a thesaurus or a book of synonyms and antonyms. You will be surprised at the wide range of words that have a similar meaning. Yet there is always a varying shade of meaning to each word. Excellent books on increasing word power are available. They can be useful in increasing your active vocabulary.

Developing one's vocabulary may appear difficult, but this not really so. It is a fascinating study that adds to your strength of expression. Words are to a student what ammunition is to a soldier. The more you have, the stronger you feel. They are the tools of precise communication.

Things to Do
1. Write the meanings of the 10 words: amplify, banquet, casual, descend, epilogue, foretell, geriatric, heredity, impulsive and juvenile. Consult the dictionary if you are unsure of their meaning.
2. Subscribe to a magazine like the *Reader's Digest*. This will improve your English.

Similar Sounding Words

The English language has many words that sound similar, but have different meanings. They can often change the meaning of a sentence or a message. Have you ever tried to differentiate between them? Their correct usage immediately reflects that the writer knows what he is trying to communicate. A good student must be aware of the meaning of each word.

Things to Do
1. Here are ten pairs of similar sounding words. Differentiate between their meanings; use a dictionary if necessary. *Adapt* and *adopt*; *bail* and *bale*; *canvas* and *canvass*; *decent* and *descent*; *eminent* and *imminent*; *flare* and *flair*; *deer* and *dear*; *hear* and *here*; *instance* and *instant*; *letter* and *latter*.
2. Write down ten pairs of similar sounding words you know.

Enjoy Words

Learn to enjoy words. Learn new words. Be clear about their meaning. It will help you differentiate between words that sound similar and increase your active vocabulary.

Even a single word can have several meanings. For example, 'dear' means beloved. It also means costly and expensive. Similarly, 'capital' means wealth. However, the word is also used to specify the city that houses the government of a state or country. The more you study each word, the better will you appreciate its meaning.

To improve language skills, learn to appreciate the finer meanings of words. It will help you become conscious of finding the right word for the right situation and take you a step closer to becoming good at effective communication.

> **Think it Over**
> *A dictionary is a must to improve language skills.*

Spellings

An aspect closely linked to the subject of similar sounding words is the use of correct spellings. You have noticed how meanings differ with a single change of an alphabet in a word, e.g. *effect* and *affect*. Both words have different meanings. Even when words are not similar sounding, the correct spelling is very important. One learns words through usage. Correct spellings too are learnt via usage. When in doubt, use a dictionary.

Punctuation

Most people think punctuation is not important and to them it is a mystery they can easily overlook. But punctuation helps make the meaning of written words clear. Most students are aware of punctuation marks, but do not know how to use them properly. There are around 30 marks, but only a few are in common use. Too much punctuation is as bad as no punctuation. The best rule in using punctuation is to use common sense.

Correctly used, punctuation adds vigour and clarity to your written work. They help separate words and ideas, group and keep together related ideas, and set aside words that need special emphasis. They are not difficult to use provided you understand their usage. Punctuation improves the clarity and effectiveness of sentences. Here is a quick look on the use of punctuation marks.

The full stop or period (.) is used:
1. At the end of a sentence.
   E.g. *Thank you for your letter.*
2. After an abbreviated word.
   E.g. *Mr., Mrs., Dr., V.P.P., C.O.D., etc.*

However, the period is no longer in popular usage with words such as Mr, Mrs, Dr and other similar examples. It is also not used:
- In abbreviations for certain organisations like: *WHO, ICAR, UNICEF, IARI,* etc.
- When the abbreviation is for a currency as *Rs, $* or *Yen.* (Some still use it for Rs, however.)
- When a name is abbreviated as *Raj* for Rajendra, or *Anu* for Anupama.
- When abbreviations such as *memo, exam* or *maths* are used instead of full words.

3. After a number or letter in an outline, such as:
   A., 1., 2., etc.
4. After a non-sentence, such as:
   Hello, good morning!
5. In groups of three (or four) when words are eliminated, as in: "*...is sturdy, easy to use and long-lasting...*"

The comma (,): This is perhaps the most misused punctuation mark. It denotes a short pause in reading and divides a sentence into divisions according to construction. E.g., *The senior schoolboys, ready for the football match, were wearing their games dress and football boots.*

It is also used to separate individual nouns and adjectives. For example:
1. *The cameras, films, albums and photo paper were dispatched through courier.*
2. *May the couple be blessed with a long, happy and prosperous wedded life.*

The comma is also used in other ways. For example, when writing the date: October 27, 2003, or after a salutation in an informal letter and the complimentary close in all cases: *My dear Raj,* and *Yours sincerely,* or *Yours very truly,.*

Use a comma whenever you feel it will make the meaning more clear. But do understand its proper use and do not sprinkle it as if it were an ornament in a communication. A good rule: whenever in doubt, do not use it!

The semi-colon (;): A semi-colon indicates a greater break in thought than a comma, but lesser than a full stop. It is best used when the second half of the sentence depends upon the first half and the two parts are connected with the word *for*. In such cases *for* can be eliminated and a semi-colon used. E.g., *We cannot accept you for this position; graduation in law is an essential qualification.*

The colon (:): The colon indicates a longer pause than the semi-colon. It divides the sentence into two or more parts, each complete in itself. It also precedes a quotation:

1. *Your salesman clearly said: "Please accept the offer as it is or leave it."*
2. *I am not surprised you let me down: I was expecting it.*
3. *Dear Mr. Arun:* or *Dear Sir:*
4. *We ordered the following: 4 cases of detergent powder, 2 cases of toilet soap and 1 case of scouring powder.*

The exclamation mark (!): This is used to express strong emotion, satire, doubt, surprise or irony. Some tend to use it excessively. If you remember it is an 'exclamation' mark, you will know when to use it. A good rule: use it sparingly. Do not use a comma in the sentence when you use the exclamation mark, e.g., *The details written by you are a great surprise. We can hardly believe it!*

The question mark (?): This is used at the end of a sentence that asks a question, e.g., *Could you advise me how I can improve my essay?* It can also be used within brackets to express doubt or uncertainty, e.g., *We expect to complete the work by November 30 (?) if peaceful conditions continue.*

The hyphen (-): This is used to join two parts of compound words, e.g., *warm-hearted; three-fifth*. It is also used with prefixes such as ex, self, all and the suffix elect, e.g., *ex-captain; self-confidence; all-India; secretary-elect*.

The dash (–): This is used to indicate a dramatic pause, e.g., *We had your order ready – in just two days!* It is also used to indicate omission of certain words or letters, e.g., *Mr. – was present in the office that day. He called him a r——l*.

Parentheses ( ): These are used when words that are not a part of the sentence are inserted into it to give an informal and confidential effect, e.g., *Your salesman (is he pushy?) was very confident about the quality of your products*.

Parentheses are also used to enclose numbers, references, directions and question marks, e.g., *You may please (1) check the balance payable by you, (2) obtain a draft for the sum on Punjab National Bank, and (3) dispatch it to us through a reliable courier. You can clear your doubts by referring to our standard terms of business printed on the reverse side of the order form (please see items 6, 7 and 8)*.

Quotation marks (" "): When certain words that are not those of the writer need to be included, they are enclosed within quotation marks, e.g., *Your salesman emphatically said, "The order will definitely be executed within a week."*

In certain cases when words are enclosed within quotation marks, they can by an expression of doubt or change of meaning of the word, e.g., *We are amused that you talked of "integrity" and "honesty"*.

Single quotation marks are used to enclose a quotation within a quotation.

Apostrophe ('): This is used to indicate the possessive case and to denote the ommission of a word, e.g., *It is Sushil's duty to look after the office record*. Or *It's time to go* is used instead of *It is time to go*. In the same way, *isn't* is used for *is not*, or *won't* for *would not*.

Ditto marks ("): These imply repetition.

E.g., 20 colour films Kodakcolour.
20 " " Agfachrome.
10 " " Fujicolour.

> **Think it Over**
> *The best way to improve your language skills is to use the language as often as possible.*

Writing Skills

Most people hesitate to write, fearing they may not be able to write well. People limit their own development through imaginary fears. The truth is everyone can write well provided one is willing to learn the simple techniques of writing. You are no exception. Believe in your personal abilities and self-confidence will help you grow.

While writing, relax. Take a rough paper. Imagine the person you wish to communicate with is sitting across the table. But he cannot hear, so you need to convey your message in writing. What is the message? Note down each point you would like to make, as if he were sitting before you and you are talking to him. Have you got all the points right? Now mark them in order of preference by placing 1, 2, 3 and so on against each. When you finally present these points to the individual, you would want to have the most important one on the top. Once you have the priorities sorted out, you can prepare the final written note.

When speaking, one can attract the attention of the other person in several ways. But when you convey a message through writing, there is only one way to attract attention – make the introduction attractive. It must arouse the interest of the other person and make him feel like reading further. He must also get to know what is being communicated.

Divide each idea or point into a paragraph. Proceed logically. Common points can be strung together in a paragraph. Write short paragraphs. They make the matter more readable. Use simple words with short sentences. They ensure crisp reading and are easy to understand. As you write, ask yourself: Is my message clear? Is it concise? Is it convincing? When you answer 'Yes' to these questions, you have done your best.

Your 'best' need not necessarily be the last word on the subject, though. Let us not forget: there is always a better way of doing the same thing. If it were not so, all progress would come to a standstill. Therefore, make it a habit to revise what you have written. Again, ask yourself: can I improve upon it? If you can, go ahead and do it. Let your work bear the stamp of perfection.

All this sounds simple. But writing in itself is a technique, which one learns only through practise. It involves knowledge of the language, good communication skills and the ability to think in terms of how others will interpret the words and expressions used. The more you write, the sooner you will learn the techniques that work. Observe the work of others. Look for the best. Adapt ideas to suit your style. Soon you will have a writing style all your own.

> **Think it Over**
>
> *To improve language skills understand the meaning of words.*

Points to Ponder

- One needs to know a language to communicate effectively.
- Every language has a vocabulary.
- Learn to use as many words as possible.
- Punctuation helps understand a message better.
- Writing skills are best learnt through practise.
- Make your writing readable. Write short sentences and paragraphs.
- The message must be clear, concise and convincing.
- With practise, develop your own writing style.

Mantra 4 : **Step 3**

Reading Skills

Reading is the first step to becoming knowledgeable. Aimed at understanding and interpretation of information, reading leads one to study. Study aims at detailed analysis of a subject or situation. This eventually leads one to become learned and knowledgeable. Unfortunately, most people are not fond of reading. Most reading is imposed upon people by their individual circumstances.

How are your reading skills? Respond to these statements by ticking one of the options.

1. I am fond of reading.
   ☐ Yes ☐ No
2. I always read with a purpose in mind.
   ☐ Yes ☐ No
3. For easy comprehension I try to understand how the book is structured.
   ☐ Yes ☐ No
4. I always adapt my reading to the type of reading material.
   ☐ Yes ☐ No
5. I read so that I can learn more in less time.
   ☐ Yes ☐ No

If all your answers are not "Yes", you need to look into your reading habits. Efficient reading can greatly improve the performance of every student.

The Reading Habit

Most people are very poor readers and not even inclined to read the newspaper. The best they can do is to glance at the front-page headlines, check if there are any interesting pictures and then put the paper aside. Youngsters reach for the sports page. Most businessmen take a quick look at the advertisements. And the family shares the Sunday newspaper, where there's something for everyone.

How many homes subscribe to magazines? Very few, indeed! Many love to borrow and read. Some read when they travel and have nothing else to keep them occupied. Very few people are regular readers. In how many homes do we see books? Most people agree that they haven't bought a book since they left college! The book industry depends largely upon the textbook requirements of schools and colleges. The percentage of the reading public is small. This lack of interest in reading reflects upon the youth, who only read school and college textbooks.

All progress depends upon development of new knowledge and its use. There is no better way of passing knowledge than through books. Therefore, if one does not want to be left behind in life one must read, read and read! There is no end to knowledge or to learning. The more you have of it, the more you want of it. Enjoy what you read. You will then want more of it.

Reading with a Purpose

We have all met people who will tell you that they love reading. Reading what? Cheap magazines! If they pick up the newspaper, they will tell you about the cases of theft, dacoity or rape. When they read magazines, they are on the lookout for gossip and scandals about film and political personalities. Even the books they read pertain to scandals and murders. The circulation of these publications speaks about their popularity.

But youngsters who have goals to achieve cannot afford to read such trash. With limited time available to reach their destinations, the reading must be purposeful. When reading, choose what appears important to you. A proper selection of reading material is essential. You cannot judge a book by its cover. Read the blurb on the back cover. Check it with the contents. Browse through the book. If you find it will help you, buy the book.

Structure of the Book

When the purpose of reading a book is to learn and become knowledgeable, the next obvious step is to discover how one can put the book to best use. Literally, there are hundreds of books dealing with similar subjects. All of them sell. But readers choose books that are easy to comprehend.

To get the best out of a book, see how it is structured. Every author has a particular style. When he is trying to provide a certain amount of knowledge, he follows certain priorities and logically presents the subject so that the reader can comprehend it step by step. Many books are illustrated. That makes understanding easier.

When a student understands how the book is structured and written, it helps immensely in making personal notes. For those who have exams looming ahead, these notes are very important. Therefore, do evaluate a book for its structure before reading it. That will make studying easy.

Adapting to Reading Material

All reading material does not deserve the same attention and time. Can a person read a newspaper word by word? If you were to try doing it, you would not complete it in a day. Again, can you read a magazine from cover to cover? Do you have that kind of time? It is just not practical since we have limited time. We read only as much as we want to and no more!

Can you read a textbook as you would a newspaper or magazine? You could, but it would be of no use. A textbook, a book being read for pleasure, a magazine and a newspaper all require different kinds of reading attention. This makes it important that the reader adapts to different kinds of reading material.

Students who have a goal to excel in exams need to read textbooks thoroughly. Similar books can be read for additional details. Magazines can be read with the purpose of updating information. A newspaper is read to increase personal awareness about the progress around the world.

Reading Efficiently

For it to be useful, you must learn a subject thoroughly. To learn well, you will need to read books well. But to read a book thoroughly one does not need to reproduce the subject word by word. It would be sufficient to read it so that one can understand the subject well.

Reading efficiency is reflected by the speed of our reading. Most of us feel we read efficiently, but it is not so. Experiments have repeatedly proved that most us can improve our reading speed by at least 50 per cent. Increasing this speed is not enough. Our comprehension of the subject must also be equally swift. Just think of how much additional knowledge you can gain by improving your reading efficiency.

Excellent books on speed-reading are available in the market. You will be well repaid for the effort you put in to improve your reading efficiency. As you learn to read faster, you will also learn to comprehend the matter faster. You will be able to do much more than what you do presently. Speed-reading is a positive step towards learning to excel in exams.

Increasing Reading Efficiency

To increase reading efficiency here are a few tips:
- Read as many books and magazines as you can.
- Be conscious of your reading speed and assimilation.
- Have a wide eye-span. Read several words at a time.
- Look for key words, phrases and ideas.
- Read groups of words instead of reading words.
- Read mentally, not verbally. Lip movements reduce reading speed.
- Assimilate what the author writes. Do not confuse it with your opinions.
- Give the subject the importance it deserves.

> **Tip**
>
> *To learn speed-reading, use your finger. Keep the finger under the printed words and move it with every word you read. Gradually increase the speed of your finger. Your reading speed will increase.*

Things to Do

1. In your study schedule list improving reading skills as a definite goal. Buy a good book on speed-reading. Study it to improve your reading skills.
2. When studying always be conscious of your reading speed and assimilation.

Points to Ponder

- Reading is the first step to becoming knowledgeable.
- Those who are fond of reading are good learners.
- Read with a purpose. Differentiate between reading for knowledge and reading for fun.
- To learn a subject quickly, check how the book is structured. Choose one in harmony with your reading style.
- Do not devote equal time for all reading material. Adapt according to need.
- Everyone needs to improve reading efficiency.
- Use as many methods as possible to improve reading efficiency.

Mantra 4 : **Step 4**

Listening Skills

Are you a good listener? Most of us are not good listeners. That may seem hard to believe, but it is nevertheless true. Respond to these statements by ticking one of the options.

1. I have always been attentive in class.
   ☐ Yes ☐ No
2. Nobody has ever complained that I did not get the full message.
   ☐ Yes ☐ No
3. If I do not understand a message I always confirm whether what I have understood is right or not.
   ☐ Yes ☐ No
4. My mind never wanders when someone is speaking to me.
   ☐ Yes ☐ No
5. I never interrupt when someone is speaking to me.
   ☐ Yes ☐ No

If the response to any of the above questions was 'No', you need to improve your listening skills.

Attentiveness

Not being attentive when a teacher is speaking means that you are not listening. You may be physically present in the class and may also be aware that someone is talking to you, but the information may be falling on deaf ears. This is more common than many of us are willing to believe. Poor listening means poor learning and indicates that we fail to understand whatever is being communicated. Is it surprising that we do not do well?

Even in everyday life people do not listen attentively. This problem is far too common than many of us believe. People listen, but without attentiveness they fail to grasp what has been said. In homes, at the workplace and even in general, lack of attentiveness means poor communication. Every person who has goals to achieve must appreciate the importance of this fact. Do not let lack of attentiveness be a cause of poor learning.

Grasping the Full Message

Few people would agree that very often they fail to grasp the complete message. For an honest opinion ask your father or mother. You could even ask your friends. They will tell you that you are absent-minded. It is very much like not being attentive in class. Listening is an acquired skill and requires you to concentrate on what is being said.

Our ability to grasp the full message depends upon the importance the message may hold for us. If it is important for us, we ensure that we do not miss the details. But if it pertains to what someone else expects us to do, we fail to be attentive and the message we receive is incomplete. After a speech if you were to make notes, you will notice that you do not have the complete message.

Confirming the Message

It is a mark of a responsible person to confirm whatever is conveyed. The habit of confirming a message must be adopted in one's younger years at school. If you failed to do so, it will still be worthwhile to develop this habit now. A responsible person does not ignore the details of anything. This is possible only when the person understands what is expected when the message is passed on. It is therefore essential that you confirm the information a person has received. When studying, you can confirm information through additional study of other books.

The Wandering Mind

A wandering mind is an important cause for being a poor listener. The normal response when someone speaks to us is to start thinking what the information means to us as a person and about an appropriate reply. But the mind cannot do two things simultaneously – listening and also thinking how to respond to the information. In a class we cannot normally speak unless asked to. We refrain from speaking, but all the same our mind switches off from listening mode and goes wandering thinking of related things! The obvious result is poor listening.

Interrupting the Speaker

One does not normally interrupt a formal speaker or a teacher, but it is common to interrupt people when a message or information is being conveyed. One may justify such interruptions saying it was necessary to confirm what was being said. This is wrong. An interruption breaks the flow of thought and speech and definitely affects the communication process.

If one needs to confirm certain facts, it is best to wait until the whole message has been delivered. Ask yourself how you would feel if someone were to interrupt when you are speaking. Since interruptions affect the learning process, one should appreciate how to use this fact for personal benefit.

What's Good Listening?

The process of listening can be divided into smaller segments for better understanding of the problem:

- **Sensing** pertains to hearing the message.
- **Interpreting** refers to understanding what has been heard.
- **Evaluating** means forming an opinion of what has been said.
- **Remembering** refers to storage of the message for future use.
- **Responding** refers to acknowledging what has been said.

What Hinders Good Listening?

Several factors affect good listening:

- **Noise:** Affects hearing.

- **Boredom:** Makes what is being said unattractive.
- **Mental block:** Does not permit a person to accept a new idea.
- **Restlessness:** Encourages interruptions.
- **Fatigue:** Diminishes the listener's concentration.

> **Think it Over**
> *The ability to listen and understand the other's viewpoint signifies intelligent behaviour.*

Becoming a Good Listener

Listening effectively is an acquired skill and requires you to concentrate on what is being said. It also requires you to refrain from speaking until the other person has finished delivering the message. Here are a few ways to become a good listener:

- Establish eye contact with the speaker. When you look at the speaker, there is an unspoken assurance that you are listening.
- Sit up with a straight back. It improves attentiveness.
- Consider how the information being provided is useful to you.
- If extraneous thoughts invade your mind, remind yourself that what is being said is important for you.
- If it is a one-to-one session, confirm what has been conveyed to you by summing it up in your own words.
- When part of a group to whom information is being imparted, nodding your head confirms you are listening. If necessary, confirm the information at the end of the session.
- When the information is important, make notes immediately after the session. It will help make the information part of your memory.

Things to Do

1. Whenever a message is conveyed to you, confirm whether you have understood it correctly. This will make you conscious of listening attentively.
2. Whenever possible, make notes.

Points to Ponder

- Most people are not good listeners.
- Lack of attention is a common cause for poor listening.
- Getting a complete message is important when listening.
- Confirming a message helps understand it better.
- A wandering mind results in poor listening.
- Interrupting a speaker affects communication.
- Listening effectively is an acquired skill.
- A good listener is a good learner.

Mantra 4 : **Step 5**

Concentration

Concentration means devoting total attention to a subject. This is important if you wish to avoid distractions and learn well. Achievements in every field have been possible because of concentration on particular subjects. Animals cannot concentrate like human beings. Even amongst humans the capacity to concentrate varies from one individual to another. But an individual's ability to concentrate properly ensures success.

Fortunately, this ability can be learnt and developed. Those who have done so assert that it begins with the breathing process. Taking the mind away from other things, think of your own breathing. Good breathing habits create harmony within a person. Breathing well depends upon one's posture.

Sitting comfortably in a chair, concentrate on your breathing. Count ten as you inhale deeply. Hold the breath. Slowly release it. As you do this repeatedly, think of the benefit the deep breathing is doing to your body. As your breathing becomes deeper, you will feel a burst of energy from within. Visualise this energy helping the finer processes within the body and making you healthy and happy, with better powers of concentration.

When you get down to studies, think of the subject just as you did with your breathing. Visualise how the study will benefit you. Sometimes one tends to concentrate deeply on one subject and not on others. In such cases, the study of one subject becomes an obsession at the cost of other subjects. This is not right. It happens when we learn to concentrate on a thing, but fail to detach ourselves when required. Therefore, learning detachment is as important as learning to concentrate.

To learn concentration really means to give your entire attention to a particular subject for a certain period and then withdraw from it. After withdrawal, you could relax or move onto another subject. This concentration helps you learn more effectively.

Things to Do

1. In a quiet room light a candle and place it a few feet away from you. Sit comfortably. Gazing at the candle, count backwards from 100 to 1. If the count breaks, start counting from 100 once again. This will teach you to bring your thoughts to one point and keep them there.
2. Make it a point not to study a subject for more than an hour. If you have to do so out of necessity, break for a few minutes after completing an hour's study.

Improving Concentration

Raja Yoga advocated by the Brahma Kumaris offers a simple yet effective technique to help quieten and clear the mind. They call it 'soul consciousness'. To achieve this, visualise a star-like entity in the centre of the forehead. Since we are all children of one father, God, we are endowed with the original nature of being at peace, love and happiness. Imagine these qualities through visualisation. Repeatedly affirm: "I am peaceful"; "I love all things"; "I am happy". When you practise these thoughts several times a day, it helps develop a peaceful mind. A peaceful mind helps you concentrate on a subject and give up negative thoughts and habits.

Points to Ponder

- The ability to concentrate ensures success.
- Your power of concentration can be improved.
- Learning detachment is as important as learning concentration.
- To improve concentration take a short break after an hour's study.

Mantra 4 : **Step 6**

Making Notes

Making notes is perhaps the most important learning process towards greater success in exams. At the school level most teachers prefer to dictate notes besides what they teach directly from textbooks. At the college level lecturers speak as students make their own notes. At still higher levels, particularly as part of self-study, people make their own notes.

What is your attitude towards making notes? Answer the statements on making notes by ticking one of the options:

1. I always make notes of whatever I study.
   ☐ Yes ☐ No
2. I find notes effective in preparing for exams.
   ☐ Yes ☐ No
3. The notes I make are clear and understandable.
   ☐ Yes ☐ No
4. I use illustrations to make notes more useful.
   ☐ Yes ☐ No
5. I never lend my notes to others.
   ☐ Yes ☐ No

If you have not answered "Yes" to all statements, you need to take a new look on making notes. You can increase your success manifold by making good study notes.

Making Notes

Everyone makes notes, but not everyone knows how to make good notes. The difference between an achiever and an underachiever is very often the way they make and use notes.

At school, many teachers dictate notes that you could rely upon and pass. These notes put you on par with the whole class. But when you wish to excel, you do not depend only upon the notes given at school. On returning home, the ideal situation is to revise what has been taught from the textbook and create notes incorporating the notes, if any, given by the teacher. This serves two purposes. Firstly, the revision helps better understanding of the subject and fixes it in the long-term memory. Secondly, the notes enable fast revision just before the exams.

What kind of exercise book is ideal for making notes? Most students use conventional exercise books and some use long books. However, an ideal exercise book for notes is the loose sheet notebook. Ruled and blank sheets are readily available in the market. The written matter can come on the ruled pages and the illustrations on the blank pages. Since the sheets are loose, additions can be made and filed at suitable places. Illustrations can also be conveniently adjusted. In certain cases, cuttings can be pasted on blank sheets and made part of the notes. The sheets can be held together in a hardcover file with a white lace. Different notebooks can be made for separate subjects.

How does one go about making notes? Most students just rewrite whatever is taught to them and make notes. That is never sufficient. To make good notes, reread the subject in the textbook. Read through the notes, if any, given by the teacher. From this information, select the matter that you feel is important. You could highlight it by underlining with a pencil. The proper selection of matter should be the first step in making notes.

What should be the criteria for selection of subject matter? The selected subject matter should make it clear about what must be learnt. Why should it be learnt? How does the information benefit you? Where and when can the information be used?

Once the matter has been selected, you cannot note it as it is. It would be voluminous. It would not serve the purpose of good notes. Therefore, the second step would necessarily be to condense the matter. Eliminate frills. Look for the essentials. That is the secret of condensing subject matter. The condensed matter can then be organised logically to make it easily understandable when one reads it later.

Most students are afraid to reword matter for fear of changing its meaning. There is nothing to be afraid of. You do not need to repeat what is written in the textbook. Reword and rephrase the matter in as simple a manner as you can. That makes it easier for you to use later. It also gives you an opportunity to write the matter in your own language and style and helps fix it better in memory.

It would also be advisable to note down other relevant information at the end of the notes. This would invariably be something you learnt earlier. Therefore, you could mention the connected information and page numbers of your notes.

Effective Notes

Notes can only be effective if you plan them so that they are easily understandable when you refer to them later. They should be logically organised. One subject should lead you to another. They should be written in a simple language just as one would explain something to a layperson with no previous knowledge about it.

Just before exams it is never practical to revise different subjects completely from textbooks. With the right kind of notes, you can revise these not once, but several times. Through notes you can review past studies, think about them and be able to answer many questions that may be asked in the exams. Therefore, to be really useful the notes should always be so prepared that one can use them as an effective tool for revision before the exams.

Clear and Understandable Notes

It is not enough to make notes; they must also be clear and understandable. Notes should be such that a glance should enable you to recall the entire subject. Good notes must be simple, well organised and easy to understand.

To highlight certain portions, you could use ball pens of different colours. The subject matter could also be broken into sections, sub-sections and even still further. Underlining is yet another way to highlight certain portions that you consider important. If you come across printed illustrations that could be useful, you could paste cuttings at appropriate places. If it is not possible to take a cutting, you could get an illustration copied on a photostat machine and then use it as a cutting.

Your personal imagination alone is the limit to the ways in which you can make notes useful. Use whatever way you wish to make the notes useful. The greater attention you pay them, the more useful your notes will be when you make revisions for exams.

Using Illustrations in Notes

Illustrations cannot be used for all subjects. However, the modern trend is to use illustrations to make the subject interesting and understandable. Illustrations play an important role in all science subjects. Even in the exams if you can supplement written work with illustrations that clearly indicate your understanding of the subject, you will definitely qualify for higher marks.

The illustration work need not only be by way of graphic representation or a picture, but can be a graph, chart, table, bar chart or even a circle divided into portions indicating percentages. Illustrations can be made more useful by using colour pencils or ball pens or even through shading with an ordinary pencil. Whatever procedure you use the idea should be to promote greater understanding of the subject.

Lending and Borrowing Notes

Shakespeare said, *Neither a lender, nor a borrower be*, for a loan loses both itself and friend. Think about it. Would you like to lose both? In class your friends are your competitors. If you wish to help them, go ahead and do so. The help should be restricted to studying together, guiding each other and offering support in general. However, study notes are the very personal effort of an individual. They are prepared to help you rise in your endeavours.

Preparing notes is very much like writing a paper on a particular subject. Would you like your friend to present the same paper like yours in class? If so, the teacher would not know who did the original work and who copied it. Under such circumstances, the obvious choice for the teacher is not to give special recognition to either student. Would you like that? Surely not! Therefore, remember that your notes are for personal use. Keep them that way.

> **Think it Over**
>
> *Writing requires more attention than reading. Making notes helps in making the subject a part of long-term memory.*

Things to Do

1. Review the notes you have been making. Consider how you can improve them.
2. Make notes for subjects on which you have no notes.

Points to Ponder

- Making notes is an important step in the learning process.
- Good notes enable fast revision before exams.
- To make notes begin by selecting the matter. Condense it. Organise it logically and note it.
- As far as possible use your own language in making notes. It will improve your writing skills.
- Notes that are easy to understand are effective notes.
- Good notes must be simple, well organised and easy to understand.
- When possible, use illustrations. It makes understanding easy.
- Notes are for your personal use. Do not lend them.

MANTRA 5

"Adapt According to Need"

Exams come in all shapes and sizes. One begins at the lowest level when little children are tested for their repetitive skills and handwriting. Gradually, the tests become harder with the student choosing objectively between two or three options, or even matching one set of objects with another.

Tests become exams and one begins to need both an understanding of the subject and the ability to put the knowledge across in writing. At the school level there are monthly tests, and quarterly, half-yearly and final exams. At each exam there may be a fixed number of questions to be answered or there may be some choice.

One begins to realise that one method is not right to tackle every exam. One is required to adapt according to need. The methods of learning have much in common. But one exam varies from another. Whereas one tests your writing skills, another may test how you comprehend a particular subject or how well you project your personality. You will need to use all your skills as you adapt according to need each time.

Mantra 5 : **Step 1**

The Wonderland of Exams

Before we consider each kind of exam in greater detail let us take a quick look at some of the common forms of exams.

Written Exams

These are the most popular form all over the world. A question paper is handed over at the beginning of the exam along with a paper on which the answers are to be written. The questions have to be answered in a fixed amount of time. The marks that each question carries are indicated. Every student is given a number that is put as a mark of identification. No names are written. At the end of the exam the answer sheets are collected, put together, sealed and sent for correction.

Practical Exams

Several subjects require practical exams along with the written exams. Subjects like Physics, Chemistry and Biology, along with several specialised lines like Entomology, Mycology, Home Science and Psychology, require practical exams. The basic purpose of these exams is to test how well a student is acquainted with equipment and procedures. Identification of samples is important. This is also an occasion to check how well the student has been doing his practical work during the period of study. A certain number of marks are allotted for the presentation of the practical notebooks.

Viva Voce

Informally referred to as viva, viva voce is an oral examination for an academic qualification. Used more at the higher levels of education, it may include a discussion on a special project or paper written by the student. Specific marks are allotted for this work, as it aims at testing the practical understanding about the findings of the project report.

Filling Questionnaires

When filling in vacancies for jobs very often written tests are replaced by questionnaires that may or may not have answer options. If answers are to be filled in, they are in the form of words, phrases or short sentences. The time allocated for these tests is short. Good general knowledge of the subject is important to answer these tests. Since these tests allow no variation in answers they are quick to assess.

Interviews

An interview is as important as the written test when the purpose is to hire personnel for any kind of vocation. This is invariably the second step in the process. The first step is the written exam. Those who qualify here are short-listed for the interview. This may be conducted by an individual, a small group of people or even by a board specially appointed for the purpose. One needs to be well prepared for these interviews. The interview provides an opportunity to project one's personality, communication skills, level of confidence and awareness of the world.

Group Discussions

These are part of the curriculum for certain admission tests and also for appointment to certain jobs where good communication skills are required. Like interviews, one is invited to participate only after qualifying in a written test. You need to be well prepared in your subject and must have the confidence to put forward your point of view.

Health Examination

A health check-up is essential for some admissions and appointments to certain kinds of jobs. This is of special importance in the defence services and for security and civil aviation personnel. Even for many other jobs where the employers offer free health services, a preliminary health examination may be necessary before being granted employment. A group of doctors does this work or sometimes it is done at a recognised government hospital. The defence services have their own hospitals.

Competitive Examinations

With millions of aspirants seeking admission into professional colleges and institutions of higher learning each year, there are a variety of exams meant specifically for selection. There are innumerable exams that lead young people to business and professional positions in almost every field one can think of. From IAS and allied services to exams for clerical positions, there is one for every need.

The Exam Industry

Exams have given rise to an entire industry that provides coaching institutions working at the national, state and local levels. It has also given rise to a big publishing industry that prints books and magazines specifically for this purpose. There is coaching at the local and personal level and even through post! Postal courses meet the need of the youth aspiring for a limited number of positions in different institutions. Good teachers are always in demand. Teachers prepare mock tests, objective question papers and model answers and also write books that simplify preparations for exams.

Besides books, study material is also available through interactive compact disks.

Are Exams Fair?

Many question the concept of exams saying they are not fair. They object to those who pass exams through unfair means. Is it fair to those who study regularly? It would be incorrect to say that exams are totally fair. There are instances of cheating in exams at all levels. If students are ingenious about cheating methods, invigilators are no less cautious in keeping an eye on such students. In every exam students are caught using unfair means and get the punishment they deserve.

There have also been instances where examiners have favoured students with low merit. This is because humans are involved in setting and checking exam papers. Human frailties will continue to create problems. Fortunately, such cases are an exception rather than the rule. Such activities soon come to light and the guilty are punished.

A Wonderland

We are indeed living in a wonderland of exams. If we wish to reach our goals, we will need to understand the set-up of this wonderland and prepare ourselves to meet the challenges that come our way. The wonderland appears like a maze through which it seems difficult to find one's way to the goal. However, when one begins to understand the many factors that impact success and prepares to face the challenges, it is not as difficult as it appears to be.

Points to Ponder
- Every exam aims at testing candidates differently.
- It is important to know what to expect in an exam.
- An entire industry caters to help candidates appearing in exams.
- Exams may not always be fair, but unfair means are looked down upon.

Mantra 5 : **Step 2**

School Exams

Exams are a regular part of the school curriculum. Every school follows a particular pattern. In most schools there are periodic tests and half-yearly and final exams. Many schools now follow the system of regular weekly tests, followed by quarterly and half-yearly exams, and then the finals. Weightage is given to the weekly tests and mid-year exams, and proportionate marks are added to the final exam score to decide promotions to the next class. This ensures that a student must be regular and performs well throughout the year.

There is a fixed syllabus for each class. Many teachers give notes besides teaching from textbooks. Students are given homework regularly so that they practise what they are taught each day. Students must revise lessons at home and also make notes.

Regular attendance at school is important. It's equally important that the homework given is completed in time. In many schools additional work is given by way of projects to be completed over a period. These must be done to the best of your ability. If necessary, take the help of elder brothers or sisters, or even parents.

Good study habits are often formed at school. Parents play an important role in enforcing these habits in the children. Even in good boarding schools where parents are not present to help children, the teachers ensure their students imbibe good study habits. Amongst other things, students are taught to study themselves, without parental supervision. These habits are a great boon in later years.

It pays to be attentive in class. Good notes are assets. The habit of visiting the library and reading other books on the subject is also very useful. Students who set goals early in life and are motivated learners always do well. They are not shy of being ignorant and dispel their doubts by unhesitatingly talking to teachers.

A good student knows his companions are competitors. All are vying for the top position. However, at this stage there is nothing at stake. If all are good students they can all qualify for special distinctions without affecting their companions. A more positive way of looking at the situation is that a student should not try to compete with others at this stage, but rather compete with himself. His aim should be to imbibe as much knowledge as possible and score better marks each time.

If a student is regular and does the prescribed work, exams should not bother him. The common rules of writing neatly, using the correct language and avoiding careless mistakes is necessary to score well. The atmosphere in the school exam hall is familiar and there should be no reason for nervousness or tension. Some pressures are always associated with exams, but those who study regularly and ensure they are relaxed need not worry about this.

> **Think it Over**
>
> *A positive learning attitude is the key to excel in exams.*

Points to Ponder
- Exams are a part of school life.
- Every school follows a particular pattern for school exams.
- Good study habits are formed at school.
- Students who study regularly always do well.
- Don't compete with others. Compete with yourself.
- Write neatly in exams and avoid careless mistakes.
- Relax before the exam to avoid tension.

Mantra 5 : **Step 3**

College Exams

As students move from school to college they enjoy their first experience of independence. Except for professional colleges and few others where they are strict and mean business, very often a student is not missed in class. This sends wrong signals to most students and they become irresponsible. Only when the attendance record is updated much later do students realise their folly.

Most college education is wasted in this country. If you do not want to waste your effort and your parents' money, ask yourself some simple questions. Do I need to go to college? Will I benefit by going there? Do I have a definite purpose in going there? Ask your parents and friends. The mental development of a college student must be above average.

Just as you have more independence to move about than you had at school, you also have greater independence to decide whether you want to study further or not. If you are in college not only to acquire a degree but also to gain more knowledge and learning so that you can rise higher in life, you will need to put in greater effort at acquiring this knowledge than you did in school.

Not many tests are conducted in college. Even when they are, not everyone is serious about them. When you want to gain knowledge, you will have to take things seriously. Firstly, get to know the syllabus you need to cover that year. Find out the books you will need. Buy them. Secondly, find out the study schedule in the college. Get to know the lecturers and professors. Attend the classes as scheduled. Thirdly, revise at home whatever is taught in college. Visit the library. Read as much as you can on the subject. Make notes. Consult your teachers whenever in doubt.

When you study regularly, you will gradually gain knowledge in the subjects of your choice. It is your personal efforts that will help you. Personal discipline will be your greatest asset.

The exams that college students look forward to are those conducted once a year by the university. As soon as the dates are announced, note them down. Have them pasted at a conspicuous place in your room – preferably on your writing desk or the corner of your dressing table mirror.

About two weeks' preparation leave is always granted before the final exams. Utilise this period properly to revise all the subjects one by one. If you have prepared good study notes, revision becomes easy. Procure old question papers from previous years. Answer them. This not only helps you revise specific subjects, but also ensures practise in writing the exam paper. This is very important as you get writing practice that will be very useful when you sit in the exam hall to answer the question paper.

When in the exam hall, read the question paper carefully, plan your strategy and answer it in your best handwriting and language. Recheck the paper when complete.

Points to Ponder
- Those who make personal efforts succeed best in college.
- Get to know the syllabus and study schedule. Work hard.
- Make personal notes on all that you study.
- Regular study ensures success.
- Utilise study leave well for revision.
- Read the question paper carefully.
- Write the question paper in your best handwriting and language.

Mantra 5 : **Step 4**

Professional College Exams

By the time students enter professional colleges they have already appeared in innumerable exams. There has been much culling of students who were unable to achieve the minimum foundation level for a career. Only those who are serious about acquiring professional knowledge and skills make it.

The atmosphere in a professional college is different from other colleges. The studies pertain to a particular line of specialisation. Besides, before specialisation a foundation of several allied subjects is necessary. Teachers are specialists in their fields. One can miss classes only at the risk of being thrown out or having to study for additional time at great cost.

Attending all classes becomes necessary. Collecting additional information about different subjects is also important. This means more frequent visits to the library and bookshops. It also means culling information from the latest magazines that write about the latest trends on almost all subjects. This, in turn, ensures it is necessary to make good notes. Therefore, after college much time is spent in this effort.

Education in these colleges aims at building all-round professionals. Much depends upon how individuals grasp specific knowledge and skills. The knowledge imparted at these institutions is not tested through one major exam, but through several smaller tests from time to time. Each step prepares the student for the next higher step.

When practical skills are also involved in the training, part of the education is imparted in special labs or workshops. Everyone is not capable of handling equipment and practical assignments, but one learns through practise. You should not hesitate to ask for help when in doubt. Very often students feel that they will not be handling such practical assignments professionally later and ignore them. This is not right. Even when these tasks appear trifling, they give an individual an insight into that particular practical assignment. This is of great benefit in life.

Just like for theoretical work, there are tests or exams for practical skills also. Both outside and in-house teachers conduct tests. Many times, special outdoor assignments are assigned to students. These require them to visit factories and business houses to work and collect first-hand information. At the end they prepare and present a report with personal inferences on different facts. The professor may hold a lengthy verbal discussion based on the report and finally award marks.

Study in professional colleges prepares students for a variety of careers. You will do well to put in your best efforts to gain the most from these courses.

Points to Ponder
- Only students who have achieved a certain foundation level reach professional colleges.
- Hard work in a variety of subjects is very important.
- To succeed one must love books and knowledge.
- Do not feel shy of learning practical skills. They can be very useful.
- Regular study ensures success.
- Put in your best effort at practical outdoor assignments.
- Aim at all-round development of your personality.

Mantra 5 : **Step 5**

Writing a Thesis

At higher levels of study where research is involved, writing the research paper, or thesis, is the ultimate exam for the student. Every student is given a specific subject for study. The information included in the research paper comes from two sources. The primary source includes information collected first-hand through interviews, actual observations and study of original documents. The secondary source includes existing reports, comments and documents written by scholars.

To collect material from the secondary source it is necessary to spend long periods in the library, reading books and journals. It is also usual for college and university libraries to stock one copy of research papers submitted by earlier students. A common tendency amongst students is to cull secondary information from earlier research papers and, with minor changes, include it in their research paper. This may seem easy, but it is not the right thing to do.

The primary information will need to be collected first-hand. The professor who supervises the student will guide you on how to proceed in the matter. When it is necessary to visit institutions or interview people, letters of introduction will be provided. When many people are to be interviewed, it might be advisable to prepare questionnaires and response sheets. Some students use a dictaphone to record conversations.

For the secondary information the student will have to visit the library. Begin your work in the reference section. You can consult a variety of encyclopaedias pertaining to the particular subject. These will not provide the actual reference material, but will impart information that will eventually lead you to the material you require. To collect the best information, refer to the original and not to condensed or abridged matter, as many students tend to. One book leads you to another.

Once you develop a lead, you will need to create your own bibliography, which is maintained best on cards – one for each entry. The card should carry the basic information about the book or the journal you refer to. Begin with the author's name (surname, first name and middle name), title of the book, year of publication and name of publisher. If it is a journal, mention the volume and issue number as well as the page numbers.

All the references you collect may not be useful. As you read them, you can write your remarks on the cards. In some cases, there will be duplication. In others, the details may be trivial. You can sort these as you read. When you make the final selection, you will have your final bibliography.

As you read the material you will need to take notes. These are best taken on loose sheets that can later be organised, as you deem best, and included in the research paper. In organising the reference material, you will need to remember the relevant questions and issues. The references may have varying opinions and you can treat them according to their relationship to your subject of study.

Once the primary and the secondary information are ready, the next step would be to plan an outline for the paper. Several samples would be available in the library. Plan it the way you feel you can project your ideas best.

The next step would be to write your paper. In doing this, remember that it is not intended to be a report of what other scholars think of the issue. The real purpose is to project your interpretation of the subject based on your primary information and the views of earlier scholars. The paper must discuss various issues pertaining to the subject and convey your complete understanding of it.

When you quote other scholars, do give full credit to them. Use footnotes for the purpose. Even when you arrive at a conclusion on the basis of your work, but you know that earlier scholars have come to similar conclusions, you can mention it in the footnotes. The author's name must come as it is and also the name of the book or journal.

As with all written communications, the report must be neatly typed and the language must be simple. There should be no grammatical or spelling mistakes. Check that the figures mentioned are correct. At the end, after your concluding observations, include the bibliography. The report will need to be bound and several copies presented.

> ### *Points to Ponder*
> ♦ At higher levels of study the writing of the research paper is the ultimate exam for a student.
> ♦ The report will include material from both primary and secondary sources.
> ♦ Begin by consulting reference books. Create your bibliography. Read original books. Collect and organise information.
> ♦ Prepare an outline and write the report as best you can.
> ♦ Give due credit to references through footnotes.
> ♦ The report must be well discussed and reflect your understanding of the subject.

Mantra 5 : **Step 6**

Know Your Examiner

There are several steps one goes through to excel in exams. It begins with understanding oneself, having definite goals, learning several skills, understanding the purpose of exams and, finally, preparing for exams. One is assessed on the basis of marks in the exams. And who gives these marks? It is the examiner – a person who corrects answer papers.

In general three individuals are involved in the exam process: the person entrusted the task of setting the question paper for the exams; invigilators who oversee arrangements for students answering the exams; and the person who corrects your answer papers.

One rarely knows the person who sets the question paper. However, one must understand that examiners frame questions according to a particular need. They are designed to test the ability of students at different levels of thinking. Questions can be classified as:

- ♦ **Recognition questions** where one needs to recognise individuals and instances through personal learning.
- ♦ **Recall questions** that test one's memory.
- ♦ **Application questions** pertaining to practical application of knowledge in particular circumstances.
- ♦ **Analysis questions** that test a student's ability to analyse a particular situation and do a detailed examination of the elements or structure of something.
- ♦ **Synthesis questions** that refer to the combination of parts to form a connected whole.
- ♦ **Evaluation questions** aimed at forming an idea of the value or worth of a situation or thing.

The responsibility of invigilators is restricted to ensuring that no unfair means are used in the exams. But it is the person who corrects the answer paper who is important to the examinee. It may not be possible to know this person's identity since secrecy is maintained in exams. However, since the marks depend upon this person, you must understand about the individual's working and expectations.

In school, your teacher corrects exam papers. Only teachers appointed specifically for the purpose correct Board Exam papers and those for competitive exams. The person who corrects your answer paper on the basis of a model answer paper receives a few rupees for every paper corrected. Therefore, the attention given to each answer paper is no more than a few minutes.

Remember this: your entire year's effort at studying the subject and three hours of answering the exam question paper receives only a few minutes of the examiner's attention! Your marks depend upon the impression you create in these few crucial minutes. You will now realise why it has been repeatedly emphasised that handwriting and presentation is very important. For an examiner who has been reading speedily through similar answer papers, presentation is an important criterion for being liberal or stingy with marks.

To reach out faster to the examiner, present an answer paper that draws immediate attention because of its neatness. Have margins on both sides of the page. Write neatly and legibly. Note down the questions as in the question paper. Start each question on a new page. Whenever possible highlight important steps by underlining them. Use illustrations if necessary. Answer those questions that you know well first. Underline the final answer or put it in a box for questions in mathematics.

When you are not completely sure of the answers to some questions, leave them for the end. You can answer these questions by bluffing your way through intelligently. For intelligent bluffing, you need to begin the answer carefully by writing a paragraph that draws immediate attention. Again, you need to have a very convincing concluding paragraph. In between, you can write whatever you know about the subject. This will not get you full marks. However, if you have created a good impression in your earlier questions, the examiner will give marks based not upon the question, but upon your general knowledge of the subject.

When writing your answers, do remember that an examiner will correct it. Your answer paper is a reflection of your knowledge and skills. Create as good an impression as you possibly can.

> **Think it Over**
>
> *Examiners do not want to know how much you know but how well you know the subject.*

Points to Ponder

- Your marks will depend upon how the examiner views your answer paper.
- Your full year's study and three hours' exam will be judged in a few minutes.
- Good handwriting and neatness speak well of a student.
- With good presentation you can intelligently bluff your way to some additional marks.
- Always write the best answer paper you can.

MANTRA 6

"Become More Competitive"

Earlier we discussed the struggle for existence in every sphere of life. It is the fittest that survive. Exams are one way of selecting the fittest persons for particular purposes. That is the reason why we see competitive exams of different kinds all over. All youngsters will need to appear in exams to prove their worth.

When we look back, we realise that all of us set goals and learnt a little more about ourselves to adopt better habits and develop skills to gain an edge over colleagues. The purpose was to become more competitive. We need to face the world. We need to forge ahead. Let us not accept others as weak. We need to plan and devise a strategy to be more competitive.

Mantra 6 : **Step 1**

Competitive Exams

There are a great variety of competitive exams that may interest youngsters seeking a career. Qualifying in some exams leads one directly into a career. In others it admits them into institutions. The entry to a career comes later.

Competitive exams aim to test a candidate with a wider perspective and expect one to possess good all-round knowledge. The syllabus covered is not restricted to a limited study. Considering the vast all-round knowledge required for these exams, the syllabus covers a big range.

Another significant difference in competitive exams as compared to school and college exams is that you are not selected on the basis of minimum marks. The number of candidates in these exams is very large and the principal aim of the exam is to select a certain number of toppers, irrespective of their marks percentage.

The ability to answer question papers with speed and accuracy is very important. This makes it necessary that the candidates are well prepared. For the best preparation for competitive exams the secret is to answer as many back papers as possible. A compilation of these question papers is available in the market. Many magazines devoted to competitive exams also publish back papers, mock tests and guidelines for success and sell sets of old issues.

Many candidates join local coaching centres that offer intensive preparation for these competitive exams. Some institutions also offer postal coaching. The secret of success lies in practise. The more one practises, the better one becomes. Even in coaching centres candidates are acquainted with as many questions and answers as possible. The candidates need to keep answering old questions to improve their response speed and accuracy.

To be well prepared the candidates must go through the recommended books in the syllabus. Good notes help you revise the study material. And additional study ensures an edge over other candidates. You need to remember that these are not qualifying but competitive exams. An edge over other candidates helps score additional marks and takes you to the top.

Good study habits developed in earlier years are the best asset to top competitive exams. Organised learning, practise, revision and a relaxed attitude help greatly in these exams.

To avoid last minute hassles ensure you receive your entry card in time. Check the location of your exam centre in advance. Also check the room where you need to sit for the exams. Since the number of participants in these exams is very large, if one is not clear about these issues well in advance, there can be great confusion at the last minute.

On the day of the examination, reach the centre in time. Be relaxed. If you have been practising on the old question papers, you should have no problem answering the exam. Write in your best handwriting and language. Before handing over your paper, check for errors and omissions.

Points to Ponder

- There are a great variety of competitive exams.
- An all-round knowledge is required to do well in these exams.
- Do remember that these are not qualifying exams but competitive ones. Only the very best are selected.
- The secret of success lies in knowing what is expected, followed by rigorous preparation and practise.
- Check the exam centre and hall a day in advance.
- Answer the exam in your best handwriting and language. Both speed and accuracy are important.

Mantra 6 : **Step 2**

Objective Type Exams

Objective type exams are common for competitive purposes. In these exams memorising or cramming a lesson does not help. To answer these, you need both knowledge and speed. These exams require short answers that may be in the form of simple words or phrases. The questions can also include sentences where the blanks are to be filled in. To create confusion, several choices may be offered. Similarly, there may be a question followed by three or four answers. You will need to tick the correct answer. Examiners keep devising new ways to test learning skills.

Most students think that answering objective type exams is easy. They do not have to think of an answer. Their only task is to choose the correct one. However, this is not true. In these exams you cannot rely only upon what has been read in textbooks. You need wider knowledge not only on specific subjects, but also on how it is linked with others. Even while choosing words to fill in blanks, you need to appreciate the finer meaning of each word.

When choosing between given answers, finer distinction between the right answer and nearly-right answers requires one to understand and analyse the specific situation. This is not always easy, particularly when you are pressed for time. The process of elimination appears an obvious choice to answer such questions. First, the incorrect alternatives should be eliminated. Second, the question can be read with the other alternatives and checked for harmony in language and sound. In this way you can arrive at the right answer.

Time is an important constraint in these exams. One may need to answer a hundred questions in an hour. That gives you 36 seconds to answer each question. Since you only need to tick a choice even 10 seconds are sufficient if you know the answer. But when you are unsure about the answer, you can get terribly confused, anxious and disturbed. This creates problems.

The best way to attempt these exams is to solve them in three rounds. Before beginning the exam read the instructions very carefully. Is there any choice? How many marks does each question carry? Are there minus marks for questions answered wrongly? After you are clear about the instructions, answer all the questions you know for sure in the first round. At the same time, tick those questions with a pencil that you can solve, but which need more time. This could be done in 10 to 15 minutes.

In the next round, answer questions that you ticked with the pencil earlier. These may require some calculations or checking. Answer them as swiftly as you can. This may take longer than the first round. Finally, get down to the difficult questions. If there are no minus marks, you can do some intelligent guessing. But do not attempt these questions if there is a risk of losing marks.

These exams are not easy. At the same time they are not very difficult either. The secret lies in getting used to solving such questions. Obtain old question papers and practise. As in all things, practise makes you perfect.

Points to Ponder

- Objective type exams are common for competitive purposes.
- These exams require all-round knowledge and speed.
- In these exams a right answer and an almost-right answer can make a big difference.
- Time is a big constraint in such exams. A swift response is important.
- Answer the exam in three rounds to obtain the best marks.
- Use intelligent guessing only if there are no minus marks.
- Practise makes you perfect. Keep trying.

Mantra 6 : **Step 3**

Pre-interview Questionnaires

Many times in between a written test and the interview there is another test. All the candidates who qualify in the written test are requested to fill in a questionnaire that seeks several additional points of information. Sometimes these questionnaires are required to be filled in and mailed before the interview. On other occasions, it is desired that the candidate bring the questionnaire for the interview.

The purpose of such questionnaires is invariably a step towards judging the attitude of the candidate. The questions are so framed that the answers reflect individual preferences, personal strengths and weaknesses. Very often the answers are used for further discussions during the interview. To understand the purpose of the questionnaires, consider a simple question that may be on the form: *Why have you opted to study in this institution?* What would you answer? Most candidates would write: "I have opted for this institute because those who pass out from here get better salaries than those from other institutions."

But consider the response from one candidate: "I have opted to study in this institute because I want the best education and I know that the faculty of this institute is better than any other in the country."

Who in your opinion would be preferred? The latter, of course! It is not that this candidate is not interested in earning money. However, his first preference is better learning, not money. His answer reveals his attitude. Besides, through his simple answer he has praised the faculty, some of whom would be interviewing him.

Let's consider yet another question that is likely to be on the questionnaire: *What are your plans after you complete studying in this institute?* Most candidates would respond: "I would like to join a good company where I can rise to the position of higher management."

In comparison, here is a response from one candidate: "After completing my education in this institute I would like to contribute to the development of business and trade through a good company so that I can experience the satisfaction of being a responsible citizen of this country."

Now, who do you think would be preferred? Again, it is the latter response that would receive immediate attention. This candidate would obviously work through a business organisation. The difference is in the attitude of individuals. What differentiates potential winners from others is their attitude of finding success by being useful to others. Their first choice is to give before receiving something in return. In most cases, the candidates take the question at face value and answer it literally. They respond to reveal what they are looking forward to. They do not realise that their success depends upon others' acceptance of their services.

These pre-interview questionnaires have many similar questions where the aim is to discover the candidates' personal hopes and aspirations, their family history, personal habits, hobbies, strengths and weaknesses. The answers to many of the questions form the basis of the interview. At this point, the interviewers would also like to judge whether the candidate has given answers in harmony with his personality or just answered with a vested interest.

Do not fill these questionnaires in a hurry. Think about the questions. Try to ascertain the purpose of the question. Write your answer in rough. Rethink it. Improve the wording, if you can. Only when you are satisfied should you fill in the questionnaire in your best handwriting. Do read the instructions on the form. Some who do not have a good handwriting prefer to type out the answers. However, it is mostly mentioned that the form must be filled in the candidate's handwriting.

If the form is to be returned before the interview, do it in time. Before mailing it, keep a photocopy for your use. Read it well before you appear for the interview. Your response at the interview and the one in the form must tally.

If you need to carry the form with you to the interview, ensure you carry it in a file. It should not be crushed. When you hand over the form to the interviewer, it should reflect the quality of your work. A good impression will carry you through the interview.

> ***Points to Ponder***
> ♦ Questionnaires are progressively being used to seek additional information about candidates.
> ♦ The questionnaires aim to judge attitudes as reflected in the answers of candidates.
> ♦ When answering the questionnaire keep the other party's point of view in mind, not your own.
> ♦ Do not fill the questionnaire hurriedly. Do it carefully.
> ♦ Keep a copy of the form for personal use.
> ♦ Let your form be a sample of your work. Make it a perfect job.

Mantra 6 : Step 4
Group Discussions

Group discussion is yet another testing medium to select students for particular vocations. A group is constituted and a subject for discussion given. One person is asked to initiate the discussion. Others follow in turns keeping within their allotted time. Good knowledge and speaking skills are important to obtain good marks.

Marks Criteria in Group Discussion

On what basis are marks given to participants in a group discussion? Candidates will do well to understand that besides speaking skills, marks are decided on several parameters. Here are a few:

1. Does the person have knowledge of the subject being discussed? How does he interpret it? Does he have creative perceptions?
2. Does the person have the ability to substantiate his arguments with good examples?
3. Does the person have analytical skills? How well does he analyse the subject being discussed?
4. Does the person have good communication skills? Besides being knowledgeable, can the person present facts and ideas convincingly?

Some of these things appear very simple. They are not! You require a lot of confidence, knowledge of the subject and proficiency in speaking to do well in a group discussion. These are important skills and one can learn them only through practise.

To do well you must understand the subject. When in doubt, do not hesitate to inquire before the discussion begins. Think about various aspects of the subject. When speaking, your opening remarks must draw attention. Substantiate statements with examples. Do not speak beyond the time allotted to you. Remember that you are under test.

Things to Do

1. To master the situation in a group discussion join a debating group in school or college.
2. Participate in declamation contests.
3. Read the newspaper regularly to be well informed on current affairs.

Points to Ponder

- Group discussions gauge the knowledge and verbal communication skills of candidates.
- A variety of skills are required to excel in these discussions.
- To succeed, speak convincingly. Substantiate statements with examples.
- Avail of every opportunity to practise public speaking.

Mantra 6 : **Step 5**

An Interview

An interview is a spoken examination for a particular position. It is an important way of putting an individual's capabilities to test. It is also an obvious next step to selecting the best persons when it is not sufficient to gauge their capabilities based only upon written exams. An interview is a test not only of an individual's capabilities, but that of his entire personality.

Purpose of an Interview

The purpose of an interview is to afford an opportunity for the examiner or prospective employer to personally gauge the individual capabilities of candidates. The written response by the candidates is never sufficient for this purpose. The interviewer wants to be sure that the candidates have the abilities they claim to possess.

Interviewers understand that an individual is not a machine that can be expected to give the desired performance under specific circumstances. Therefore, it becomes necessary to gauge an individual's abilities with the particular purpose of how well they can be put to practical use. In an interview, an important purpose is to gauge whether the individual understands his subject, is an eager learner, flexible in his attitude and capable of handling a variety of situations that the knowledge of his subject may require.

Types of Interviews

Depending upon the circumstances and the need, a person could be interviewed in several ways. One must understand how to face them:

- ♦ **Telephone interview:** This would be a one-to-one conversation on phone. In all likelihood, it would be at an appointed time. The best you can do is speak cheerfully and confidently.

- **Preliminary interview:** This is a screening process after the written test. Important questions may not be asked at this step. However, one needs to be at one's best to qualify for the final interview.
- **Panel interview:** Everyone is well aware of the interview where a panel of experts ask questions before selecting a candidate. In these interviews your personality and body language are important, as you are under complete observation. Have a smile on your face and maintain eye contact with the interviewers. Stay calm under all circumstances.
- **Sequential interview:** Instead of a panel comprising experts from different departments, candidates are asked to move from one department to another where the interviewer asks questions. In these interviews, the personal whims and fancies of the interviewer matter. The candidate will necessarily need to be careful about this.
- **Skill-based interview:** In vocational institutions skill-based interviews are important. The candidates may be asked to actually perform in a mock sale or other situation. At such interviews, the candidates must be fully aware about the expectations of interviewers.

Preparing for the Interview

If an individual qualifies in the written exam, the obvious next step will be to receive an interview call. Do not waste your time until the all-important letter arrives. Instead, begin preparing for the interview. It is going to be an important meeting for both you and the interviewer or prospective employer. For you, securing the job or a particular qualification depends upon it, while for the interviewer it is an occasion to assess your ability and know how you can fulfil his interests.

To understand the needs of your prospective interviewer better, find out all you can about the organisation – its set-up, branches, products and services. If you can, also find out all about the responsibilities and privileges of the position you have applied for. Such information can be collected from advertisements in the national press, advertising literature, journals, local distributors and even local retailers. Information about other similar organisations can also prove useful. Thus equipped, you will be in a good position to understand and answer important questions during the interview. However, if the interviewer does not show any interest, do not try to impress him with your knowledge.

When you finally receive a call for the interview, you should immediately acknowledge it, confirming the place, day and time mentioned in the letter. Have your file containing the original documents mentioned in your application ready. If you are working, you may have to apply for leave well in advance. Although it is natural for ambitious young people to search for better positions, many employers do not like this. Therefore, you need not mention this as a reason for seeking leave. It is perfectly in order to ask for leave to attend to personal matters.

During the interview, the interviewer would like to confirm facts you may have mentioned in your application. He will also want to gauge your knowledge, special interests and achievements, the ability to learn new skills and your willingness to work under specific circumstances. The ability to make decisions is vital to many jobs and he may want to judge your ability in this direction also. The interview will afford him an occasion to assess your general image. Interviewers are particularly interested in the health and personality as exhibited by one's poise, manners and sense of dress. He may also inquire about your past successes and failures, and how you faced them. Your reactions and answers to the interviewer's questions will help him conclude whether you suit his requirements or not.

Things to Remember

When invited for an interview, do remember one special purpose is to judge your body language. You can mean one thing and say quite another. However, one cannot do this with body language. It always sends out true signals about you. The way you shake hands, stand, walk and sit speaks volumes about you. Your gestures – crossing your arms, placing them on the side or letting them rest in your lap etc – are also important. Making eye contact or avoiding the gaze of the interviewer reflects your confidence level. To project a good image, smile, appear cheerful, walk confidently, sit erect and make eye contact with the interviewer. If you cannot do this, practise it. It will make a great impact on your success.

Why Candidates Fail in Interviews

Many candidates wonder why they failed in the interview. Here are some common reasons you need to be aware of:

- Not being aware of the purpose of the interview.
- Appearing late for the interview.
- Appearing in shabby clothes or ones not ironed.
- A casual dress and attitude.
- Lack of good manners.
- Poor communication skills.
- Poor knowledge of the subject.
- Unrealistic aspirations.
- Discouraging body language.
- Lack of self-confidence.

Some typical questions asked during interviews:
1. Tell us something about yourself – your family, education and expectations?
2. Why do you wish to join our organisation/institution?
3. Would you like to be with us on a short-term or long-term basis?
4. Have you any plans for the future?
5. What kind of work do you like: desk job or fieldwork?
6. Have you applied to some other organisation?
7. Do you have any hobbies?
8. Are you computer-literate?

The Interview

You must reach the interview venue punctually at the appointed time. Be appropriately dressed. Do remember that you are not going for a picnic or a fashion show. Wear a neat day suit. If the weather or the circumstances do not permit, a white shirt with a coloured pant and a necktie would be appropriate. Wear either brown or black shoes to match. Make certain you have shaved, clipped your nails and have properly groomed hair. Original certificates and documents must be carried in a neat file. Do not tuck them in your pocket or in an ugly envelope stuffed into the pocket.

When you arrive for the interview, do not try to get friendly with the receptionist or the other candidates, and start comparing notes and qualifications. Do not overlook the simple fact that they are your competitors. Do not smoke. You can spend your time until you are called by reading a newspaper or a book. If you prefer to read a book, do not read cheap fiction. Your interviewer may be reading this too, but when it comes to candidates, interviewers prefer the latter read constructive books.

When you are called for the interview, do remember that a good first impression is important. Take a deep breath and enter with a smile. This helps dispel nervousness. Wish the interviewer 'Good morning' or 'Good afternoon', depending upon the time of day. Sit down only when asked to. Let the interviewer begin the conversation. He will probably begin by asking you questions to which he already knows the answers. This is to put you at ease. Gradually, he will come to more pertinent questions. These will be intended to assess your personal ability. He will want to hear you rather than speak himself, but never interrupt the interviewer. Hear him carefully and then answer clearly and audibly. Do not use slang words or smoke, even if the interviewer offers you a cigarette.

If you have mentioned some special interests and achievements in your application, the interviewer may want to know more about them with particular reference to how they affect your hopes and aspirations. While talking about your special interests, give them only that proportion of your attention as is fair compared to the interests of the interviewer. Family circumstances may also crop up in the interview. When the interviewer encourages you to express your opinion about a particular problem, do not take advantage of the situation to discuss your personal philosophies or show that you are learned and clever. Answer to the point in simple language that conveys the correct meaning. Do not forget that your communication skills are on test.

The interviewer may want to test your reactions in special circumstances. To do so he may ask provocative questions or broach controversial subjects. Such occasions demand great tact and patience. Do not be provoked under any circumstances. Display complete cool and discuss your viewpoint with a smile.

All interviewers have an eye for discrepancies. They will positively ask you reasons for past failures and shortcomings, if any. Under such circumstances, do not try to fool the interviewer. Explain your viewpoint soundly. If you are changing jobs, explain that soundly too. Do not blame those with whom you work presently. It would be more acceptable if you were to say that the circumstances do not suit you, rather than that your present employer has made things difficult for you.

If your interviewer asks you about a subject you do not know anything about, do not be afraid to confess your ignorance. If it is something vital you do not know about, you can still express your ignorance and apologise for it. Your sincerity will be appreciated.

Interviewers are also humans and may have their own whims and fancies. At the same time, they have an eye for people with ability. They will not immediately disclose whether you have qualified or not. Before concluding, the interviewer may ask if you wish to know anything in particular. You can avail of this opportunity to clarify doubts, if any, but be extremely brief and specific.

> **Think it Over**
>
> *In an interview do not speak too fast or too slow.*

Success at the Interview

To succeed at the interview ensure you understand the exact purpose of the interview. Plan your own strategy to ensure that the particular purpose is fulfilled. Follow the common rules that have been explained. You don't have to blow your own trumpet, but remember that just as the interview is an occasion for the interviewer to judge you as an individual, it is also an opportunity for you to sell your accomplishments to the interviewer. You need to project yourself as you are. You need to assure the interviewer that accepting you will benefit him.

Points to Ponder

- An interview is a spoken examination for a particular position.
- The interviewer uses the opportunity to gauge the personal capabilities of candidates.
- There are several kinds of interviews.
- Advance preparation for interviews is always beneficial.
- Body language is important in an interview. It speaks loudly about you.
- Little slips can doom an interview.
- Projecting a positive image at an interview is important.
- An interview offers a candidate a good opportunity to sell his capabilities.

Mantra 6 : **Step 6**

Medical Examination

A medical examination is a check-up of an individual's health. In many competitive exams, besides the written tests and interviews, a health examination is equally important. The principal reason for a health examination is that certain health standards are necessary in some vocations. This is particularly so in the defence services, police service, the aviation industry and several such vocations. Even in the private sector where companies provide medical benefits to employees, they insist upon a health examination before granting employment.

What can a candidate do to ensure success in a medical examination? The answer is simple. You must maintain good health. This means being health-conscious. You must appreciate the need for nutritious food, ample exercise and good habits. Young people who participate actively in outdoor activities enjoy good health. However, despite an active disposition, few people appreciate the need for good eyesight that's required in certain vocations. It would be worthwhile to be sure that all is well.

To ensure success in the medical examination, do not wait until the last moment. Visit a doctor and check that your weight is in proportion to your height. Check your blood pressure and breathing. Good eyesight is important. Candidates have been rejected for colour blindness, a fact unknown to them. This may require a visit to an eye specialist. If the doctor advises it, you could also have an X-ray of the chest and a urine and blood examination.

The purpose of this preliminary check-up is to ensure that it is worth the while preparing and going through the initial written exams and the interview. There are instances when, after having qualified in tests, candidates were declared unfit on the basis of the medical examination. This can be very disheartening. So, do not ignore this exam until the end. Do it now.

Points to Ponder

♦ A medical examination is a test of one's health.
♦ A medical examination is mandatory for several vocations.
♦ Individuals who are physically fit do well in the medical examination.
♦ A preliminary health check-up can be useful in avoiding disappointment at a later stage.

MANTRA 7

"Give Off Your Best"

When a person knows the destination and oneself, and develops necessary skills to adapt to the needs of a particular situation, the final step is to give off one's best. The purpose of an all-round preparation is always the same – to be able to perform well.

To perform well, everyone wants to know whether there are any aids available to make things easier. Will there be any hurdles in the way? What about anxiety and tension? Does everyone experience it? How can you prevent them from lowering your performance? Coupled with these problems is the need to know how to best utilise the time allowed for making preparations.

Finally, there comes a time to give off your best. This brings success. You finally achieve what you set out to do – excel in exams!

Mantra 7 : **Step 1**

Aids to Better Preparation

Considering the number and variety of exams that are conducted each year, there is a complete industry catering to the needs of people appearing in exams. Hundreds of thousands are employed in keeping this industry moving. Can any of the study aids help you perform better in exams? You will need to answer this question keeping in view your own circumstances. The principal aim of this industry is to provide aids that help you prepare better for exams. Several ways are suggested. You will need to understand them before you can use some of these personally.

Coaching Classes

Since teaching in schools and colleges is based upon a syllabus that aims at mass teaching, it does not always serve to prepare one for a specialised competitive exam. To overcome this shortcoming, a variety of coaching classes exist not only in bigger cities, but also in small towns. Coaching classes are big business. We have them at the national, state and local level. Some provide postal coaching also. The basic aim of these classes is to provide intensive preparation via rigorous practice.

The charges for some of the coaching classes can be high. Before you enrol, scout around a little. Visit the institutions in your area. Talk to the students. Seek their candid opinions about the teaching staff. Ascertain the fees. Sometimes these are negotiable on one pretext or another. Ensure you get the best deal. Whichever institution you join, there is no guarantee that it will ensure your success. What is important is how you take advantage of the training and, through rigorous practice, prepare yourself for a particular exam.

Magazines on Competitive Exams

The market is flooded with magazines for students who are preparing for competitive exams. Many are available in college libraries. Most bookshops that sell textbooks also stock them. Very often students subscribe to one magazine each and share them within their group.

These magazines carry details of forthcoming exams, articles that tell you how to prepare for certain exams, mock tests and a variety of questionnaires and old questions that can be used for practise. Old issues of the magazines may be available at special rates. You can subscribe to a magazine that suits your particular need.

Exam-related Books

Just like magazines, a variety of books related to exams are available. The subjects may be as varied as books for the CBSE or for post-graduation courses or for the IAS and Allied Services.

These books can be useful in preparing for exams. However, very often the danger is that many students rely entirely upon these books rather than studying textbooks that are a part of the syllabus. These books discourage students from making notes. For this reason the learning is not as good as it should be. Many students do pass the exams depending upon these books, but without a complete study and personal notes, it is not possible to excel in exams.

The Internet

The Internet is a great source of information and knowledge that did not exist a few years ago. Although school children are using computers as much as others, their interest may be limited to schoolbooks. However, the Internet provides an opportunity for a lot of knowledge. Even those who do not have computers can use them at cyber cafés.

Try to locate your study interests at one of these sites:
- www.howtostudy.com
- www.mathgoodies.com
- www.free-ed.net
- www.rivendel.com

- www.worldwidelearn.com
- www.allexperts.com

Any kind of study aid is definitely a support to help you excel in exams. But no aid is a replacement for personal study and hard work. A good rule: use an aid whenever you can, but do not depend totally upon it.

Points to Ponder
- A vast industry provides study aids for students.
- Some coaching is essential for competitive exams.
- Choose a coaching institute with some caution.
- Magazines can be useful for competitive exams.
- Do not depend entirely upon exam books.
- There is no substitute to practise and hard work.

Mantra 7 : **Step 2**
Exam Anxiety and Tension

All exams cause some anxiety and tension. This is true not only for youngsters, but equally so for adults appearing for different exams. The principal cause for such anxiety and tension is fear of failure. Failure is associated with humiliation and nobody likes to feel humiliated. Not even little children just starting out in school. From the positive angle, this anxiety and tension is good in that it motivates people to work harder to avoid the humiliation of failure. But from the negative angle both anxiety and tension create health problems. Digestion may be affected. One may become forgetful or suffer sleep disorders.

Everyone appearing for exams needs to be conscious of both aspects of anxiety and tension. These vanish when a person enjoys self-confidence. This in turn comes from self-discipline and better preparation. We have discussed these earlier. For developing greater self-confidence, the best way is to practise learning the subject or skill.

Even when a person's first priority is academic success, recreational activities of all kinds are important to get rid of anxiety and tension. Equally important is the need for rest and relaxation in between these activities. Earlier, we have also discussed the need for proper sleep. For all who wish to stay free from the negative effects of anxiety and tension, it is important to have a well-planned work schedule.

At a time when everyone is looking for instant relief, students wonder if certain drugs could be useful to relieve anxiety and tension associated with exams. These drugs could provide some relief, but are not advisable for use by youngsters. Students need to appear for exams periodically. If they begin to use these drugs, it can lead to problems of drug abuse and addiction.

Deep breathing exercises, outdoor games, meditation and prayer help relieve anxiety and tension. Even indoor games and hobbies are very helpful. Watching TV, movies or listening to good music relieves tension. Since every individual is unique, and different things create a variety of responses in individuals, everyone must decide what is best in given circumstances.

Points to Ponder
- All kinds of exams cause anxiety and tension.
- The fear of failure is the principal cause of tension.
- Tension has both positive and negative effects.
- To avoid negative reactions, one must learn to cope with tension.
- Have a work schedule that includes tension-relieving activities.
- Never compromise on rest, relaxation and sleep.

Mantra 7 : **Step 3**

Preparing for the Exam

In some schools and almost all colleges it is customary to provide preparatory leave before exams. This leave – usually for two weeks – must be utilised for the purpose that it has been granted: preparing for exams.

This is the time to revise all that you have learnt. Note down the dates and precise time when the exams are scheduled. Have the list displayed at a prominent place. For each subject, check that the syllabus has been fully covered. Have textbooks and notes ready subject-wise. Evaluate your own preparedness for each subject. Do you need an equal amount of study for each subject? Or is extra effort required for some subject?

Since these two weeks are to be utilised totally for revising your learning on the subjects, you will need a new schedule of study. In planning the schedule, follow the rules discussed earlier. Do not study a subject for long periods. And alternate subjects to avoid boredom. Have brief periods of rest and relaxation. Do not forego sleep. Do not allow tension to build up. Do not treat this period as a do-or-die situation. Lead a normal life. Only the additional time at your disposal is to be used for study at home. It is important that when you appear for the exams you are relaxed and confident.

If you have been following the techniques discussed earlier you will be reasonably well prepared for the exams. If you have been making personal notes, revision becomes easier. Browse through textbooks after you read the notes on the relevant subject. Do not confuse yourself with additional study of books. Since exams have to be written, do not totally spend the time reading. Do include some writing work daily. If you do not write for two weeks, by the time you appear for the exams you will find writing difficult due to non-practise.

If you are appearing for the exams in an institution you are not acquainted with, you must visit it at least a day before the exams. There are always cases of last-minute confusion and you cannot afford to let that happen to you.

The last one or two days of the leave must be exclusively used to revise the subject of the first exam. Close the revision in the evening before the exam. Have your pens, pencils and other necessary items ready. Make sure that you carry an extra pen. If a water bottle is permitted, carry one. A few sips of water in between the exam are refreshing. Go to bed early. You can wake up earlier the next morning. Have a bath and get refreshed. If you want a quick revision, check your notes. An hour or so before the exam do nothing. If you feel tense, breathe deeply to relax yourself. Crack jokes with friends. Stay calm.

With one subject less to study after the first exam, get down to preparing for the next exam. If time permits, use the period immediately after the exam for deep relaxation. Take a walk, meet friends or watch a programme on the television. Once you feel relaxed, begin revising for the next exam.

Think it Over

In an exam a balance between speed and accuracy is important.

Points to Ponder
- Use preparation leave to revise your knowledge.
- Prepare a schedule of study exclusively for this period.
- Alternate subjects of study. Include reading and writing assignments.
- Do not permit tension to build up.
- Be relaxed and at ease when you appear for the exam.

Mantra 7 : **Step 4**

The Exam

On the day of the exam make sure that you rise early, get ready, collect the necessary items and reach the exam hall well in time. Do not confuse yourself at this stage by discussing anything with friends. With a few minutes to spare visit the restroom, drink water and stay calm. Be at the gate of the exam hall five minutes before the scheduled time.

Once you enter identify your desk and settle down. Mark your name or roll number on the answer paper. Ensure it is clear and legible. Fill in any other details, if necessary.

The Question Paper

Do not begin answering the question paper the moment it is handed over to you. It is true that you have limited time at your disposal and every minute counts. But the time spent reading and understanding the question paper is well worth the five minutes you need for it. More marks are lost through wrong reading or interpretation of the questions than through any other cause.

As you read the question paper, if you think it is easy, do not get excited. If you think it is difficult, do not get confused. Keep your cool. As you read through, plan your strategy. How many questions are there on the paper? How many of these are to be answered? Do not choose in a hurry. Think about it. What would be in your favour? How much time is available to answer each question?

Time management is important. For example, if you have to answer five questions in three hours, that is 180 minutes, you have 36 minutes precisely to answer each question. Of the total time, take away five minutes for reading and understanding the question paper. Take another 15 minutes for revising the answers at the end. That leaves you with 32 minutes per question. Under such circumstances, it would be advisable to allocate 30 minutes to each question. The balance

10 minutes can be utilised as a cushion of extra time required for a longer answer.

When students read the questions, the tendency is to spot the subject of the question. Students wish to decide how well they know it. However, the important consideration should be what the examiner wants to know about the subject. Mark key words in the questions. Here are a few typical key words and phrases:

- Explain in detail...
- Compare and contrast... and...
- Prove that...
- What is your opinion about...
- Write short notes on...
- Discuss in detail...
- How would you explain...?
- Briefly describe...
- Differentiate between... and...
- Compare... with...
- Describe...
- Give examples of...

Examiners have their own ways of drafting questions. It is the little catches in the wording that matter. Look for key words. It is for you to understand what the examiner really demands through the question. This is possible only when you read and understand the questions correctly.

Writing the Paper

Once you have understood what the examiner desires, you can start writing the answers. Leave a margin on the left side of the answer paper. You could draw lines with a ruler and pencil to make uniform margins. For convenience you could write the question at the beginning. If it is time-consuming you could directly write the question number as in the question paper. After giving an appropriate title to the answer, start writing.

It is needless to repeat it, but... *use your best handwriting*. Your writing skills are on test. Use appropriate words. Mind your spellings. Use correct punctuation marks. Write as though you were explaining the subject to a person who knows nothing about it. Write an attractive introduction. Follow it with the subject matter point by point divided into paragraphs. Conclude with an emphatic ending.

Keep an eye on your watch. If you are able to finish the question in 25 minutes, instead of the 30 minutes allotted, let it not make you guilty. If you find midway that you will not finish the answer in the allotted time, cut short the details somewhat, but do not miss out on the points you have in mind. Conclude the answer like you would do normally. Let it not bother you unduly if you exceed the allotted time by a few minutes. The cushioning will absorb these extra minutes.

If a question has several parts – as for example: Write short notes on... – and there are four subjects that need to be covered, you will need to answer the question in the same 30 minutes allotted to it. Condense your answers so that you could write each note in 7 to 8 minutes each.

Unless you keep within the allotted timeframe you will not be able to write the answer for all the five questions. If you miss out on one, you have voluntarily lost 20 per cent marks. No student who wants to excel in the exams can afford to do so. Keep your eye on the watch.

A problem contrary to the one of writing too slowly to complete all the questions in time is that of trying to finish answering the questions before time. Some try to write as though they are in some sort of race. Writing fast will only be at the cost of quality. No additional marks are given for being efficient and finishing before time. Therefore, take your time. If you have a few minutes to spare, recheck the paper. Make sure you have not left out anything.

If you need to illustrate some answer with a diagram, it will have to be done within the allotted time. The diagram may not be very accurate in the short time available.

However, it must be explanatory and assure the examiner that you know your subject.

When you have completed the answer paper, recheck it for errors and omissions. Careless mistakes account for the loss of a lot of marks. Check and recheck. If corrections have to be incorporated, do so neatly. Only when you are convinced that you have put in your best effort in answering the question paper should you hand over the paper to the examiner.

Problematic Situations

Sometimes it so happens that an examinee has not taken enough rest and, when faced with the question paper, may become totally blank. This is a serious situation from the examinee's point of view. Immediate relief can come from sucking on a lozenge or sweetmeat, taking a few sips of water and breathing deeply. Complete relief comes only with rest, relaxation and sleep.

Even when the situation is not acute and limited to forgetting what you have learnt, breathing deeply and drinking water helps. Since the mind is the central controlling organ, the basic problem stems from lack of self-confidence and inadequate preparation for the exam. For relief you will need to follow the long-term preparations discussed previously.

After the Exam

When the exam is over and the students meet each other, the first temptation is to compare answers and discover how well one has done. Avoid this as far as possible. Once the answer paper has been handed over, nothing can be done. Making comparisons often causes confusion and doubt. This can be very discouraging at times and will affect your performance in the next papers.

The best thing to do after the exam is to go home and relax. If you want to check how well you have done, do it on your own. Assess your personal performance. Thank God for whatever you have been able to achieve. Keep yourself in a high level of motivation. You need to revise and prepare for the next exam.

Points to Ponder
- Arrive at the exam hall well prepared a few minutes before the exam.
- Read the question paper carefully. Look for key words in the questions.
- Time management is important if you want to score well.
- Put in your best efforts to answer the question paper.
- Use illustrations wherever necessary.
- Beware of problematic situations.
- After the exam, just relax and go home. Don't compare notes.

Mantra 7 : **Step 5**
Success in Exams

There is no single formula that can make you successful in exams. Success in exams is dependent upon several little details put together.

If you follow these seven mantras, you will succeed every time. You are aware of your destination. You know of your own abilities. Over a period of time, when you develop reading, listening and other communication skills, you develop study habits that make you a winner each time. Good habits last a lifetime.

Exams will come in a variety of types and situations. With your newly developed skills you will be able to adapt yourself to the changing needs of different exams. A positive attitude, a high level of motivation and the will to put in your best efforts will ensure success every time. Miss out on any of the seven mantras and you will feel insecure.

Sometimes when you do not meet your own expectations, do not let it worry you. It is natural to become overconfident with preparation. This overconfidence may take you unawares and confront you with failure. Nobody fails unless one admits failure. Minor ups and downs are part of life. Let them not dishearten you.

Keep innovating. Always be on the lookout for better ways to do everything. There is no place for anxiety or tension. You have goals to achieve. You have a long way to go. You will need to be determined to succeed.

With a winning spirit there is no reason why you should not excel in exams. Keep going. Work hard. Success awaits you. Best of luck!

www.ingramcontent.com/pod-product-compliance
Lightning Source LLC
Chambersburg PA
CBHW070334230426
43663CB00011B/2315